ISBN - 978-0-578-03294-8

Dedication

I wrote this with the support of my loving husband Peter Haggerty and my brilliant students, to those of you new to the ideas of performance presented within, I say

"Welcome to the family"

Special thanks to the NTID Performing Arts Department colleagues who have used this material and have helped me refine the information:

Aaron Weir Kelstone, Thomas Warfield, Damita Peace, Gerald Argetsinger, Jeanette Giagios, Bonnie Meath-Lang, Joseph Bochner, Lynn Hayes, Joe Hamilton, Erin Thomas, Jim Orr, Mark Benjamin

Anything especially good in these pages can be credited to their careful assistance, anything incorrect is completely my own.

TABLE OF CONTENTS

Patricia McAllister gets instruction from Dr. Haggerty during *Windows of the Soul*
Photographer: Julie Busch

Troy Chapman, Katie Lechner, Igor Djenje in "Sign-Arella" Photographer: Erin Thomas

CHAPTER ONE: Performance Guidelines

Important Elements of Drama
(please dress for class in a way that allows you to move comfortably - similar to a dance class).

In its purest form theater is a representation of real life within a living moment and by studying this discipline you can allow your own personality, thoughts and judgments to quiet, and the joy that is brought by the flow creativity through humanity can be experienced and expressed.

The characteristic dimensions of a positive acting experience allowing spirit to flow:
1. Clear goals: The script will guide you on where you hope to go with the character. You can also expect immediate feedback by the director which allows for a person to know instantly how well they are doing.
2. Opportunities for making a decisive action are high and that action is matched by skill. Personal skills are suited to the challenge and you are not asked to do something you are not ready to do.
3. Action and awareness blend so that the mind can quiet and focus on the single goal of communicating the message.
4. Concentration on the task at hand; irrelevant worries and concerns are temporarily suspended.
5. the actor feels a sense of potential control
6. The actor has a loss of self-consciousness, transcendence of ego boundaries, a sense of growth and a sense of being part of a larger entity.
7. Often an altered sense of time; which seems to pass faster than normal.
8. If all of the above are in place the sense that the work is worth doing for its own sake is at the heart of the experience.

Consider the message

Acting is not successful if it becomes a selfish act, it must remain a communication in a living moment between the actors and the audience, which conveys a message that has some importance to both. The actor is not the only person with responsibility. The role of audience member is to welcome a willing suspension of disbelief. More simply put, the audience willingly allows themselves to consider the story, movement and acting real even though they know they are not. If the actors are not believable or the play has a conflicted message the illusion is broken and the enjoyment of the work is lost leaving the audience member feeling disappointment that they provided their half of the communication but the theater people didn't allow them to enter into the moment.
If you are unable to find the strength to inhabit a character that may be very different from yourself, think about your audience and your hope to inspire, educate or uplift their perspectives.

1. Choosing a space – is the audience comfortable, can they sit, see and hear your story without discomfort?
2. Choosing material – is the topic relevant? Interesting? New? Current? Understandable?
3. Is your theme or message clear and is it consistent with the sensibilities of your audience? Very often a play that was written for a specific audience (for example: Broadway) and for a specific time period (for example: "Raisin in the Sun" pictured below left: Mia Sanchez, Troy Chapman. Photographer: Julie

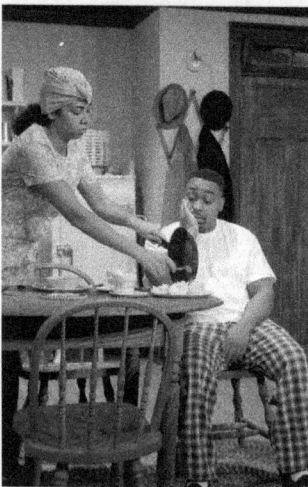

Busch) has great artistic value whose merits might be lost if the audience is in conflict with minor aspects (for example: language choices). Most playwrights change their work as it develops throughout the run of the play. When a published play comes into our hands it is the result of what worked well for a specific audience, with a specific cast of actors at a specific time and place in history. But, drama is a living art. Recognize that your cast of actors has specific strengths to be highlighted, your audience has specific concerns and your time and place also alter the original work. Therefore, if direction or actor interpretation can better enhance the play's message in this day and age it is an appropriate artistic choice to create a production that best shows this piece of literature to this audience – not simply recreate an accurate replica of how it worked in the past.

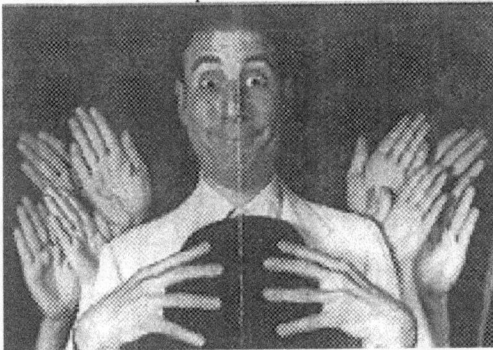

Roy Doliner in "Motion Poetry" Photographer: Carl Sturmer

DID YOU KNOW?

Silence can speak louder than words
When actors read a script for the first time, they often state the lines clearly and without pause. But, take a moment to observe how people express themselves in real life, they stall as they search for the right word, make vocal "music" (ahh, hmmm, oh, wellll). Sometimes conversation stops altogether while the parties reflect on what was just said. Conversely, the human mind works amazingly fast and there are times when in a living conversation people interrupt, speak faster or inaccurately. Feel free to play with the lines – add accents, pauses, or vocal music

1. 90% of human communication is through body language, facial expression and gesture. Words are only 10% of the message
2. posture – high center of gravity implies a character that is intellectual, center of gravity at the chest is an emotional character and low center of gravity – through the hips creates the appearance of a physically based character
3. eye contact is the actor's greatest tool, you guide where the audience will look by what you focus on – don't waste that "spotlight"
4. movement – shifting or rocking for no reason is distracting to the audience, be sure that your movement supports what you are doing with the character (youth is usually graceful, strength is agile, old age is stiff, childish is continuous and nervous movement
5. facial expression - generally the rules for basic expression are learned by children, but cultural or familial habits might cause miss interpretation – practice with a mirror or video camera to insure that your wide open smile conveys happiness (not a snarl) or your stoic look is more than simply neutral. More than half of acting is REACTING your facial expression can imply a line even when you don't have words.

6. body direction/orientation – turning away from someone shuts off communication, so many actors tend to face their scene partner, but this means you are turned away from the audience – be sure to keep them in your communication and don't shut them off.

Actor's Ethics

In the co-operative world of theater no individual actor is entitled to a private system of ethics. It is important to understand these rules of etiquette so that you are better able to work within the team.

(Troy Chapman, Quinn Cruise in "Othello" Photographer, Erin Thomas)

1. punctuality and dependability – acting is a very vulnerable activity, if the people who work with you learn that you can't be trusted that will end up hurting your ability to have a relationship with them in character as well as in real life. In theater it's always a good idea to be EARLY.
2. Speaking/signing clearly and loudly – even if you are a shy person you are more likely to get negative attention if you force the audience to strain to hear you or understand you – remember acting is not about YOU its about the message and communication with your audience.
3. Rehearsals are for everyone. Sometime people feel that they personally don't need to rehearse any more – they know their lines and blocking. Rehearsals are NOT for individuals they are for the entire group. When you are absent it means you have made it impossible for someone else to rehearse. Also, the work is never done, very skilled actors are always finding ways to keep the work fresh and new. It is also important to know what is happening to the characters you relate to in scenes that you may not appear in. Really valuable information can be lost if you "disappear" when you are not personally on stage.
4. The most interesting part of the body is the face – be sure you give the audience your face as fully as possible – not your profile or your back!
5. Be sure that you are always involving the audience. Theater may have some "secrets" (special effects) but it shouldn't have games played by the actors which are unrelated to the message. Someone you know is ALWAYS in the audience, give them the best show you can.
6. Take care of each other – in real life we are often alone or undefended, stage is the one place where that never happens, you always have your family of actors around you. Honor that tradition, if someone drops a line, cover for them, if they have their back turned to the audience step downstage to help them remember to face the audience. When you make each other look good the entire experience is elevated when you don't help each other, it simply becomes work.

7. Honor the audience's suspension of disbelief, when you "break" (laugh on stage) you insult the audience and their trust in your portrayal of the character. There is no such thing as "he makes me laugh" it is your own lack of focus or shallow character development that leaves you open to feeling your self on stage seeing a friend (not his character) on stage.
8. There is no such thing as perfect. In "live" theater costumes get misplaced, people make wrong entrances or say the wrong line. Very often it is the clever way the actors can make the mistake seem "right" that create memorable performances. Just as we strive for perfection in life, we work hard for it on stage, but when things go wrong, what will be remembered is not the mistake but how you handled it with grace and patience.
9. You will only be able to do on stage what you rehearse. Only very inexperienced actors think that they will do what they imagine – you will do what you DO. Every rehearsal helps you put the action into acting. Use it fully!

(Luane Davis Haggerty & Thomas Warfield in "DanceQuest" Photographer, Damita Peace)

Exercises for skit building

The Where Game –
Have the students split into groups. Let them discuss locations – kitchens, libraries, bedrooms, classroom, office (etc.). What are the important pieces of furniture in those rooms? Have each member of the team enter and through mime establish one piece of furniture in the room.
Evaluation – the other team should be able to guess where they are. Switch and play again.

What's Beyond?
Play again only this time the actors should suggest through movement or by talking with each other what went on in the place (off stage) that the player left in order to come into

the room. (example – coming inside after shoveling snow, getting the morning paper, walking the dog etc.)
Evaluation – can the scene partners adjust to the information the entering actor gives them and build on it?

What's Next?
Play again only this time the actors should suggest through movement or talking where they are going.
Evaluation – is the goal or destination clear enough to be understood without someone saying specifically where they are going?

(Mir Ayaz Ali, Idalia Vasquez, Karrifth Norman, Martina Bell, -kneeling- Karla Martinez, Troy Chapman, Luane Davis Haggerty leaving NTID for NYC appearance on "law & Order" episode titled "The Silencer" Photographer, Peter Haggerty)

Exercises for character building

"Safe Place to play"
Observe how people naturally arrange themselves in the room and comment
"without thinking you constantly adjust your relationship to the space to make yourself feel safe and comfortable
1. wander around the space, to find your best place to work
2. Find the places that are uncomfortable as well as comfortable
3. Move (sit, kneel, roll, jump) in that space.
4. Middle of room, near a wall, in the light? In the dark? Facing others? Facing away?
5. Find your space to begin your warm-up
6. Let yourself be aware of how you knew which place to choose

" not physicality for it's own sake-but physicality because the body serves as a pathway into our emotional life and as a means of knowing and expressing what we feel."

The goals of the exercises below include: Control (safety) and awareness of moving between external and internal

Stream of consciousness warm-up – do your own warm-up – calisthenics, dance, Yoga whatever. Then as an emotion appears physicalize it – mind is racing – run, depressed huddle, happy jump.
Don't judge, don't try to stop your mind from wandering – simply notice your mind's activity.

Circle - debrief (sweeping clear your mental attic - not cleaning, just leaving space to begin the work)
Mind is fast- body can't keep up, some are trivial, some can be used.
Bring your mind to your body OR bring your body to your mind

- **Breathing together:** in this exercise, the leader begins by making eye contact with someone in the circle the leader then exhales as the person who they are looking at inhales. The person who has now received the breath initiates a new contact, first eyes and then breathe. As the group becomes more relaxed, be sure they know laughing is allowed and the breath can start to have context and response. For example the first person mimes smoking a cigarette and blows the smoke at the second person who receives the breath by coughing, that person turns the cough into blowing bubbles and the person who receives pops the bubbles with a finger, the finger becomes a dandelion stem and the breath is sent with the mimed dandelion fluff and so on. This exercise brings the group together; each person is honored and given attention. An effect of the exercise is that the whole group begins to breathe together and focus together as they focus on the individual.

Note: breathing exercises are a foundation of Yoga, Tai Chi, emotional grounding and speech exercises all used for centering the actor, and creating a calm centered place from which to begin the process of breathing life into a character. In Deaf culture eye contact, the length of time directly shared and the withholding of eye contact are part of the relational foundation.

- **Handshape Hand-off:** The leader chooses one hand shape, for example, a full open hand, as you might use in the natural gesture for "stop" then each member of the group uses the same shape but to convey a different meaning. In the introductory stages, it is all right to allow actual American Sign Language Words to be expressed with that hand shape; but at more intermediate levels, it should become a universal gesture or mimed movement. At more advanced levels, each of the shapes should connect to form a complete thought produced by the whole group and should be a communicative gesture.

Note: hand shape and gesture are clearly foundation elements of American Sign Language. Using the hand shapes in this way parodies a Deaf children's game of poetic language play (Padden and Humphries 1988:91). It is also similar to the Meisner acting game of taking an actual object–a pole for instance, and having each actor use it in a different way (Meisner, 1961:10). Michael Checkov discusses "molding the space around the actor" (1953:8)

- **MPG: Movement, posture and gesture:** The entire class lines up on one side of the classroom and one by one each person crosses the room using a different kind of movement (skipping, crawling, hopping, short steps, long steps, tip toes, etc.). No one is allowed to repeat the same kind of movement. Once on the other side the challenge is to add a different posture to the movement you originally chose (expanded, contracted, center of gravity low, high or in your torso). After all are done the last cross adds in a gesture (universal "Hello", "cry", "you/me", "stop" etc.). Last time across have everyone define a character who might represent themselves that way. Does it remind you of how people move in a particular type of job? Is it human? Spirit? Animal? Magical? Have the actor continue to represent that MPG until everyone has found a satisfactory identification of character. This exercise can be done in reverse to enhance character analysis too – name a character like "Little red Riding Hood" and ask the student to represent her movement, posture and gestures. This can also be used as a framework for observational work. Watch the people around you copy the MPG of three people known to the class (teacher? Sports hero? Political figure?)

Note: This method was refined while teaching courses at the National Technical Institute for the Deaf and was suggested by the students themselves. It is a blend of mask work and translation process.

Acting I 2010 Spring final performance in the Dyer Art Gallery at NTID.

Homework assignment #1

Visualization
Why it's so important to visualize your character....
Probably first described by Anton Checkhov, visualization is, in many ways, essential for all great acting. The character you play is usually not like you. Your character is the writer's vision of someone else. That means the character does not have many of your characteristics. They don't have your smile, your eye color or your nervous tick. They don't walk like you, move like you or dress like you. Therefore, in order for an actor to perform a character believably, the actor must "see" their character's behaviors and try to embody them.

Each and every time you get into character and prepare for acting, be sure you first imagine seeing your character when you look in the mirror.

See: Age, body shape, profession, location – don't over analyze

What your character is wearing?
When we wear fancy clothing, we tend to feel cool, confident or even sexy. When we wear tattered clothing, we tend to feel less so. Choosing the right clothing for the character makes the actor feel more in tune with how the character is supposed to feel. Whatever you are actually wearing – visualize the style of dress your character might have on.

What your character is thinking at various times in the script?
What is the character thinking at various times of the script? Seeing the way he or she behaves in various moments helps piece together how the character is to react when confronted with various stimuli. Everything is based on how the character interprets what is being said – a simple hello at the wrong time might be an insult!

How does your character move?
The way we move says an awful lot about who we are. Walking tall and proud with shoulders back conveys the exact opposite message from walking slow and slouched. The way a performer conducts movement for the character, so too, tells the story of who that character is and what he or she is thinking and feeling.

How does the character react to certain stimuli? Pick a situation where your character would react in an extreme way and explain it.
See if the character, for example, is an introverted or extroverted person? If introverted, he or she might react to receiving some bad news by becoming more withdrawn, while the extrovert might erupt with rage.

The character's miscellaneous movements.
Does the character rock back and forth a lot while speaking? If so, it might help portray a character who is unsure of himself. Small movements can achieve huge results.

Many times your unconscious movements will create a physical "white noise" interrupting stage presence.

Assignment for the next class:

Professor Haggerty will assign you a "character type" . Between now and the next class notice real people who are similar to that type in any way. You will be asked to improvise in this character and be prepared to hand in your answers to the questions on this paper. Please type your answers to the chart on a separate page.

Playwright (the writer of the play) Shanny Mow uses P.I.M.P. to create a character. See if you can use that too.

P = Physical Describe their looks	What does your character look like? It might be very different from how you look naturally.	
I= Idiosyncrasies Imagine some habits	What habits make your character unique? Smoker? Nervous? Forgetful? Positive person?	
M = Motivation What are their goals	What would make your character work harder? Love? Money? Respect? Do guess – give reasons why that is their goal	
P = Psychology How do they believe the world works?	What does your character believe? Religious? Not religious? Paranoid? Over confident?	

Extra Credit: Research Shanny Mow and write a two paragraph biography.

CHAPTER TWO: Mask Work

(Luane Davis Haggerty, Ph.D teaching at NTID (left) Photographer, Peter Haggerty)

This form of acting style uses what is called "mask imaging" to create characters. Simply put, it means using outward physical appearance as a tool for actors, teachers, and performers to help in character creation and storytelling. During class you will be creating your character and then designing your mask. It is expected that you continue to bring the mask to class until we are finished exploring this type of acting. The masks used for the class are primarily the neutral acting masks forcing the student to use their body language and gesture to convey emotion rather than using the face.

In our next unit we will discuss physical acting styles including "commedia del Arte". You will need your mask for that unit as well and I will be asking you to design your mask to conform to "commedia" type. This type of mask is designed to work with the actor's face, transforming it, but leaving part of the face exposed. This type of mask allows the actor to combine the physical appearance of the mask, with the expressions of the actor's own eyes, brows, body, and/or mouth-- the conscious and unconscious elements of the actor's psyche, as manifested in speech and body language. But for now we will focus on the neutral mask.

The overall transformation that can be achieved with masks is powerful for both the actor and the audience, making it a natural tool for effective communication and expression. Masks and costumes have played a central role in religious ceremonies and rituals since the Stone Age, they are used in every culture and country. Masks have incredible importance to our culture and religion today

The point of using masks in acting is to explore the idea that, we all control our feelings and reactions which become a form of psychological "masks" of all sorts whatever we do for a living. Whenever we change so much as our facial expression, select glasses, or trim our nose hairs. Understanding that power--no, not the power of nose hairs, the power of masks--and making that power work to your advantage (or perhaps to less of a disadvantage) is the goal of this unit of the course. (Below -Students in the NTID 2009 Fall Acting I Class, Photographer, Luane Haggerty)

Feelings Are A Matter of Degree

The challenge in mask work is to be able to create believable emotions using your full body Practice creating the emotions below with your actor's "neutral" mask.

	Happiness	Depression	Anger	Fear
Subtle Emotion **The 1-2-3 feelings**	• Relieved • Refreshed • Glad • Pleased • Amused • Content • Optimistic • Calm • Composed • Comfortable • Cool	• Flat • Bored • Discontented • Resigned • Apathetic • Numb • Blue • Gloomy • Low • Sad • Down • Bewildered	• Peeved • Bugged • Annoyed • Ruffled • Harassed • Irritated • Irked • Frustrated • Put-upon • Resentful	• Shy • Startled • Uneasy • Tense • Concerned • Timid • Apprehensive • Cautious • Pensive • Up-tight
Middle **Emotion** **The 4-5-6-7 feelings**	• Delighted • Joyful • Merry • Ticked • Glowing • Festive • Frisky • Spry • Happy • Proud • Joyous • Excited • Cheerful • Giddy	• Disappointed • Slighted • Drained • Disheartened • Hurt • Ashamed • Depressed • Lost • Regretful • Ignored • Burdened • Rotten • Lonely • Unhappy	• Disgusted • Ticked-off • Mad • Smoldering • Riled • Pissed-Off • Hot • Contemptuous • Animosity • Jealous • Fed-up • Mean • Spiteful • Angry	• Alarmed • Jittery • Scared • Frightened • Fearful • Threatened • Trebly • Shaken • Anxious • Worried • Nervous • Afraid
Intense Emotions **The 8-9-10 feelings**	• Elated • Ecstasy • Blissful • Sparkling • Overjoyed • Radiant • Wonderful • Fantastic • Exhilarated	• Miserable • Crushed • Helpless • Humiliated • Worthless • Abandoned • Overwhelmed • Hopeless • Lifeless	• Enraged • Fuming • Burning-up • Furious • Incensed • Infuriated • Destructive • Hate-filled	• Dread • Panic-Stricken • Terrified • Horrified • Petrified • Shocked

AN INTRODUCTION TO MASKS

Mask is a form of disguise. It is an object
that is frequently worn over or in front of
the face to hide the identity of a person
and by its own image represents another
being. This essential characteristic of
hiding and revealing personalities or
moods is common to all masks. As
cultural objects they have been used
throughout the world in all periods since
the Stone Age.

A mask is anything used to hide, protect, or cover part or all of the face. Masks are worn as a part
of a costume or a disguise. Some masks are worn to protect such as a catcher's mask in baseball
or a gas mask. Most masks worn to disguise are in the form of an animal or another person.
Protective masks serve a specific purpose. For example: a welder wears a steel mask with special
glass to shield their eyes from the intense light produced by welding rod. Disguise masks include
ceremonial masks, theatrical masks, burial and death masks, and festival masks.

Since at least Paleolithic times people have used masks. Made of wood, basketry, bark, corn
husks, cloth, leather, skulls, papier-mâché, and other materials, masks may cover the face, the
entire head, or the head and shoulders, and they are sometimes considered part of an
accompanying costume. Masks vary
widely in their realism or abstraction, their
use of symbols, and their ornaments. The
kachina masks of the Pueblo peoples, for
example, have only minimal facial
features, whereas masks of the Native
Americans of the Pacific Northwest are
often elaborately carved and painted, may
have movable jaws or other parts, and
may even open to reveal a second mask
beneath the first. Occasionally, a mask is
not intended to be worn on the face, for
example the enormous ritual masks of
Oceania and the tiny fingertip masks of
Inuit women. (Masks pictured right from Dyer Art Gallery, Photographer, Robert Baker)

****Please take the time to look up different masks from different cultures on the internet. Print out one example and be ready to explain it to the class.

RITUAL MASKS:

The dancer who wears a mask in a ceremony is frequently believed to be transformed into or possessed by the spirit inhabiting or represented by the mask. Masks are often believed to contain great power, being potentially dangerous unless handled with the proper rites. The process of making a mask may require its own ritual. For example, Iroquois false-face masks, must be carved from a living tree. When making the mask the artist must ask the tree permission. Ritual masks generally depict deities, mythological beings, good and evil spirits, spirits of ancestors and the dead, animal spirits, and other beings believed to have power over humanity. Masks of human ancestors or totem ancestors (beings or animals to which a clan or family traces its ancestry) are often objects of family pride; when they are regarded as the place where the spirit lives. Many masks are believed to have magical powers, for example; the fearsome 6-m (20-ft) high totem masks of the Papuans of New Guinea are believed to frighten away evil spirits and thus protect the living. Totem, ancestral, and other spirit masks are frequently used in initiation ceremonies, and the initiation masks of West Africa are renowned for their beauty.

In agricultural rites (ceremonies designed to assist farming), masks may represent rain or fertility deities; similarly, animal masks may be worn in ceremonies to ensure a successful hunt. Shamans throughout the world wear masks in curative rites. In East Asia and Sri Lanka, masks may be worn to protect the wearer against (or to cure) diseases such as measles and cholera. In some cultures, masked members of secret societies (such as the duk-duk of New Guinea) terrorize wrongdoers and thus enforce social codes. In parts of Africa, legal judgments are pronounced by masked judges; a historical European parallel is the masked executioner. In festivals in Mexico and other countries, masks may be used for entertainment, storytelling, caricature, and social satire. Grotesque war masks were worn in battle in ancient Greece and Rome, in medieval Japan, and by the Northwest Coast peoples of North America; today, war masks survive chiefly in ceremonies.

(Image right show a detail of a Grecian Baccanalia mosaic showing masks. Image courtesy of googleimages)

In funeral ceremonies, masked dancers may seek to drive the soul of the deceased into the spirit world, where it will not harm the living. In memorial rites, masks may be worn to represent departed personages or ancestors. Occasionally, as in pre-Columbian Mexico, masks may be placed on memorial statues. Burial masks are sometimes placed on the face of a corpse (for example, by the Hopi people and in ancient Egypt, Rome, China, and Mexico), either to protect the deceased from evil spirits or, as in Egypt, to guide the dead person's spirit to its home in the afterlife. Death masks, made from wax impressions of the features of the deceased, were used in Egypt and Rome as models for sculpted portraits. In medieval Europe, the death mask itself served as a memorial effigy; this use, for famous persons, persisted into the 20th century. We still use masks in our own culture during Halloween or Carnival.

THEATRICAL MASKS

Ancient Greek drama was semi religious, rooted in masked ritual. The masks worn by actors in Greek plays were large, with conventionalized features and exaggerated expressions; the wide mouth of the mask contained a brass megaphone to help project the actor's voice to the large audiences. These masks fell into two general categories, tragic and comic, with many variations for both types. In Rome, masks were used in comedy and by pantomimes. (Photo left from New Orleans mask shop, photographer Peter Haggerty)

In the mystery and miracle plays of medieval Europe, masks were used to portray dragons, monsters, allegorical characters such as the seven deadly sins, and, inevitably, the devil. The actor portraying God frequently wore a gilt mask. During the Renaissance, half masks covering the eyes and nose were used in the commedia dell'arte; these masks are the apparent ancestor of the modern domino mask, which covers only the eyes. Masks were employed in Renaissance courtly entertainments such as the masque and the ballet de cour, and they survived in ballet until the late 18th century. In modern Western theater, masks are used mainly to represent animal characters, although occasionally a playwright or choreographer experiments with masked personages, as in The Great God Brown (1926) by the American dramatist Eugene O'Neill.

In Indonesia, masks are used in village ritual dance dramas and in dramas derived from shadow-puppet plays. The traditional pageants and religious-didactic plays of China required masks representing kings, princesses, and grotesque characters, and the mystery plays of Tibet feature masked players representing demons and other spirits. In Japan, the most famous use of masks is in the No plays; made of lacquered or gilded plaster by highly respected artisans, No masks are admired for their subtlety of expression.

But we begin our class with neutral masks

(see acting class 2008 on right, photographer, Peter Haggerty)

BASIC MASK WORK

(Dr. Haggerty teaching masks (left)
acting class NTID Fall 2008 (below), photographer, Peter Haggerty)

Never put on or take off your mask in front of the audience unless you intend to make the character appear to only be in the mask. The audience needs to see the whole picture of you AND the mask to believe in the character; not see them attached separately.

Because most of us are raised watching television and movies with many close up images of faces, the acting work most copied by young actors is facial and doesn't use the entire body. With mask work your face doesn't move so all of the emotional communication must be done physically. As you practice representing physical emotions with you mask some guidelines include the MPG (Movement, Posture, gesture) method touched on is an earlier homework and expanded here:

1) **Moving** across the floor:
Tempo – fast, slow, moderate
Articulation – bouncy, sharp smoothly
Strode – short (tip toe), long (taking up a lot of space, exaggerated)

2) **Posture**:
Expanded – standing tall, chest open

Contracted – hunched over shoulders down

3) **Gesture**:
Articulated (detailed use of finger)
Blades (full hand fingers together)
Fists (clenched palms)

Mask Quiz
Please type your answers on a separate sheet of paper

What kinds of ceremonies or rituals use masks?

1)
2)
3)

Describe how you show one character while in a mask by describing your

Movement (how you walk across the floor)

Posture (how you stand)

Gesture (what do you do with your hands?)

Which character did you describe?

When you act as a character why do you need to give yourself a context (or a full story – not just a name but who they are, who they know, what they are doing etc.)? Use an extra page if you need more room to write.

Watching everyday people and trying to copy what you see is a good way to learn how to represent a wide variety or people. What do you do when you want to copy how another person walks, talks and reacts to things (do you mimic the? Write it down? Take a picture? A video?)

True or False:
The script gives you all the information needed to act a role _____

The actor of a line always communicates clearly to the listener through words ___

Body language and facial expression is 90% of all communication____

Gestures that are in conflict with the test are confusing ____

Gestures that support the text are redundant ____

You must always be graceful in stage movement ____

Emotional subtext is clearer through body language ____

Masks are not used in professional theater today ____

Costumes and make-up can be used as an actor's mask ____

Use this space to explain one new discovery (or skill) you found out about while studying acting through the use of masks.

CHAPTER THREE: Physical performance techniques

As acting developed we moved away from the need to have a costume or mask and moved into ways to physically represent a character. Beginning with the stock characters of Italian Commedia del Arte and continuing with Elizabethan styles of declarative acting these basic approaches to representing a character are still useful.

Commedia's stock characters:
- Pantalone (a lecherous miserly, old villain)
- The two lovers
- Dottore (foolish peasant always involved in his neighbors affairs)
- Capitano (bragging soldier)
- Zanni (comic servants)
- Harlequin (clever lower class character who can fool upper class rulers)

Pictured below -Karen Kinbar, Luane Davis, Frank McAllister, David Hastings, in a commedia production of NUTCRACKER AND THE MOUSE KING for IRT, Photographer, Carl Sturmer

Try to notice how these standard or stock characters appear in modern drama.

Standard "lazzi" or bits – still used in comedy today (think of the Marx Brothers, Three Stooges, Laurel and Hardy, Dumb and Dumber, Adam Sandler etc.)

- The Statue - while pretending to be a stature the character evesdrops on a conversation and plays tricks on the other characters when their backs are turned.
- Hands behind back – while actor #1 has his hands behind his back actor #2 gestures for him (slaps, pinches his nose, rude gestures to other characters that must be explained etc.)
- Somersault with wine – extreme physical moves while carrying a fragile object, trips, falls, acrobatic moves happen without breaking or spilling the object.
- Innocent bystander – two people argue and a third tries to break them up, the third character ends up being beaten by both of them

- The chair – pulling out the chair just as someone is about to sit (usually "unconsciously" not malicious)
- Eating the fly – catch a fly study it for a moment and eat it.
- Eating cherries – a background character eats cherries and throws the pits at a leading character, the audience sees what is happening the lead character doesn't.
- False arm – the character is arrested or caught and escapes by leaving the false arm with the apprehender
- The chase – one character chases another but both remain stationary on stage, miming running and making threatening gestures at one another
- The script – the character tells a joke to the audience (no laugh) he tells it more slowly (still no laugh) consults the script and either re tells the joke in a different way or rips out the page and throws it away.
- Nightfall – the characters behave as if they are in total darkness. This allows opportunity for mistaken identities, tripping over furniture (and each other) and other comic business.

"Speak the speech I pray you" – Hamlet

Elizabethan styles of acting became more natural; remember at the Globe Theater in London the audience was very close to the actors and posing wouldn't sit well. The audience was also used to telling the actors aloud during the performance if they believed them or not. Some physical staging techniques still used are:

- Fencing and careful stage combat that is energetic, intense and realistic.
- The Bow – formal placing the feet apart the bow includes knees, hips, waist and head – removal of the hat if there is one. An informal bow involves only the chest and head but still removal of the hat if there is one.
- Curtsy – one foot far behind the other, the lower the bow the higher the person being addressed. The bounce curtsey is used on quick exits.
- "Dumb show" - silent acting which is slow exaggerated and precise to differentiate it from the "real" action.

Photo: Cynobia Demps, Gaila Williams "Midsummer Night's Dream", Photographer, Carl Sturmer

Most theater using stylized work requires some knowledge of physical approaches to acting

1773 Denis Diderot:
The actor who has nothing but reason and calculation is frigid. The one who has nothing but excitement and emotionalism is silly. What makes the human being of supreme excellence is a kind of balance between calculation and warmth.

1881 Francios Delsarte:
"Gesture is the direct agent of the heart, it is the spirit of which speech is merely the letter."
"A perfect reproduction of the outer manifestation of some passion , the giving of the outer sign will cause a reflex within." (Stebbins)

Names and introductory exercises of important creators of physical techniques:

The actor in training today can chose from many different disciplines. It would be easy to get overwhelmed with the different techniques and performance styles that are available. Some are based in physical expression some in alignment and awareness of the body, others are focused on mask work or clowning. Some of the familiar forms of physical theater or movement training include physical characterization, spatial relationships, ensemble work, improvisation, games, mime. The opportunities for the Deaf actor have never been richer.

According to David Bridel while writing for the American theater magazine (1/11/11)

"Regardless of their differing emphasis, all modern theatrical movement systems for the actor agree that the imagination is the engine of the actor's physical life."

Therefore, those actors who believe that yoga, dance class or a visit to the gym is all the preparation needed to prepare your body for acting need to think again! Here are some snapshots of the best known modern physical acting techniques used in professional theater today.

Jacques Lecoq (1921-99) remains one of the primary sources of movement training in American. Known directors who are attracted to this method include: Peter Brooks, Julie Taymor and Geoffrey Rush. Lecoq stressed the importance of external forms – architectural, musical and theatrical. He based his work in anthropology, the study of gesture and the anatomical study of the body. Lecoq embraced the form of the traditional clown (red nose, topsy-turvy dress). (Photo right – J. Lecoq, Lincoln Center Library - public domain)

Sample Exercise: Throw an object into the center of the room. Allow the students to see where it lands, then ask them to close their eyes and search for the shoe until they find it. Have the observing students describe the range of emotional responses the active student had – confusion, confidence, surprise, achievement, disappointment, etc. That range of emotions can then be applied to a scene or dialogue.

Tadashi Suzuki – A modern Japanese director who borrowed elements of Noh and Kabuki theater and translated them into a more contemporary naturalistic style. He felt the actor should develop their own style under pressure. Less thought and more action so placing the actor in discomfort, or requiring them to present and exercise with little or no preparation is part of this style. It is often a faster way to help an actor reach a breakthrough and growth. Although it often is uncomfortable, for example, if an actor freezes in rehearsal and can't think if their next line Suzuki would insist that everyone wait (not help or improvise) and allow the actor to struggle through until they came to a way out of the problem themselves.

(photo right- students prepare a monologue Suzuki style, 2011 NTID Acting class)

Sample Exercises: statues – recite a short monologue while maintaining a pose. Beginners can choose their own pose as you get more advanced the poses follow the traditional tai chi pattern. Three "unnatural" shapes to take hold of, sharply freeze, and recite - contracted, laying out, expanded.

Rudolf LaBan (1879- 1958) – He believed that movement or dance links the actor to emotion, the use of instinct allows access to the unconscious. He focused on four main categories: body, effort, shape, and space. The body category describes structural and physical characteristics of the human body while moving. Effort, or what Laban sometimes described as dynamics, is a system for understanding the more subtle characteristics about the way a movement is done with respect to inner intention. The difference between punching someone in anger and reaching for a glass is slight in terms of body organization - both rely on extension of the arm. The attention to the strength of the movement, the control of the movement and the timing of the movement are very different. It is important to remember that all categories are related, and Shape is often an integrating factor for combining the categories into meaningful movement. Space from LaBan's perspective involves motion in connection with the environment, and with spatial patterns, pathways, and lines of spatial tension. Laban described a complex system of geometry based on harmonic (visually pleasing lines or images)

LABAN
EFFORT GRAPH

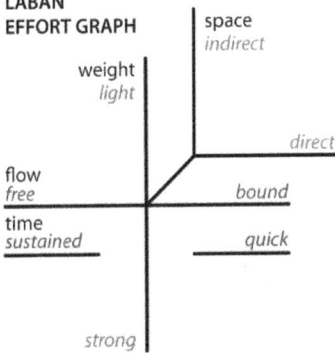

space
indirect

weight
light

direct

flow
free

bound

time
sustained

quick

strong

Sample Exercises: gesture play, by using various movements to take over the whole body you can inform a character. Begin in silence with (for example) a wringing gesture, twisting your wrist, reaching out and pulling back, change the tempo – faster or slower. Now using that motion recite lines and make the character "wring" example Malvolio in Twelfth Night as he finds out Olivia doesn't love him, twisting waist, bent knees etc. you can "wring" the entire character.
Other gestures – punch, slash, open palm etc.

(Graph left from Leban Movement group Worskhop 2011)

Delsarte (1811-1871)- Delsarte chose to continue to study what he called, The Natural Laws of Expression. He spent time watching people in all types of situations, children at play, wives waiting for word of their husbands after a mine collapse, deathbed watches, etc. All this to see how people naturally expressed themselves. He found that there is a common physical form of communication regardless of language or cultural background. He broke his findings into the Law of Trinity also a metaphor for his own Christian beliefs.

"The unity of three things, each of which is essential to the other two, each co-existing in time, co-penetrating in space, a co-operative in motion. Many religions have the concept of the Trinity, most notably the Father Son and Holy Spirit. So it is with representing life. In the case of the performance it is essential TO KNOW, TO DO AND TO BE."

(Delsarte quoted in T. Shawn [1954] *Every Little Movement,* Whitmark and Sons, NYC)

Photo left: Vivian Hasbrouke, David Rosenburg, Norman Danzer "A Flea in Her Ear", Photographer, Carl Sturmer

Through his observations he discovered certain patterns of expression, eventually called the Science of Applied Aesthetics. This consisted of a thorough examination of voice, breath, movement dynamics, encompassing all of the expressive elements of the human body. Delsarte's work inspired modern dancers such as Isadora Duncan, Ruth St. Denis and Ted Shawn. Rudolph Laban and F. Matthias Alexander also studied Delsarte's teachings until they later developed their own methods.

Delsarte never wrote a book explaining his method firsthand, and neither did his only protégé, actor Steele MacKaye. However, MacKaye's student Genevieve Stebbins did write a book in 1885 titled *The Delsarte System of Expression*, and it became a wild success.

Sample Exercise: Have the students stand as tall as they possibly can (center of gravity high - intellectual) ask them to maintain that posture and walk across the floor – observe what happens (shorter steps, feet placed closer together) Discuss how that makes the actor feel to move like that – do they know of anyone who naturally moves that way?

Have the Students feel the center of their weight placed in the chest (contracted or expanded - emotional) have them move across the floor and go through the same observational and discussion process and they did with the first placement of gravity.

Have the students place the center of gravity very low - through the floor (Physical) again have them move across the floor and observe and discuss who this affects the emotions (internal) and the reactions of others (external).

(graphic right from ted Shawn's "Every Little Movement" public domain)

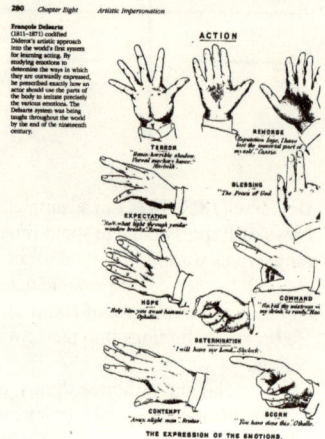

Some additional modern physical styles that are considered respected and effective include:

Parkour – a physical discipline in which the actor attempts to negotiate obstacles in his environment in the most efficient way possible. Jumping, running, vaulting, climbing, balancing. This is sometimes called extreme sport in the media. While Martial Arts addresses the human fight response Parkour address the flight response.

Action Theater – Created by Ruth Zaporah this is an approach that plays with ensemble sound and movement to reach inner depths of character. As the ensemble warms up breathing patterns and percussion can be made into musical compositions. Movement plays with timing, position and shifts. This all ultimately applies to the content of a script with conditions, situations that inverts the relationship between body and page.

Decroux – places the actor at the center of the creative process. The actor's make all the decisions about what should appear on stage. An example of the process is if you were to want to perform a "tree" on stage , in Method you would feel the tree and so look like a tree. In Decroix you observe the tree, analyze it scientifically, replicate the movement and the audience should feel the tree. Much of this training involves puppetry work.

(left -Dr Haggerty explains movement 2009 Acting class)

(Right -ASL Poetry Society Workshop participants 2010)

Homework #3
This is an open book quiz – please use your textbook to answer the questions below. For added credit use an addition page to add in more detail from your work in class.

The stock characters in commedia del'arte are:
1)
2)
3)
4)
5)
6)

Tell me a little these famous teachers of physical acting techniques:

Suzuki

LaBan

Delsarte

Describe one "lazzi" –

Describe one form of period movement from the Elizabethan era –

True or False:
Many styled theater pieces use physical acting techniques _____
Most physical styles of acting are old fashioned _____
Only clown or buffoon characters use physical acting _____
If you work in TV or movies you don't need to know physical techniques _____
If you prefer psychological acting, physical techniques get in the way _____
You can expand your versatility on stage through physical acting _____
We all have a physical accent _____

Watch and observe a physical situation in real life. It might involve a mis-communication, an ironic moment, an embarrassing moment, a surprising situation. Describe the scene; type your description.

Scene Title:

Describe the characters involved:

Setting (where are they?:

When did it happen?

What was the situation just before an action took place?

Explain the action (the problem)

Describe the event:

How did it end?

Use your description of this "lazzi" as a script, gather your actors and perform the scene for class. Make up any needed dialogue and video tape it.

CHAPTER FOUR: Monologue Preparation, Photo/Resumes And audition tools

MONOLOGUES

A Monologue is a *Mini-play* with just one actor. It is one way an actor can show his or her talent without having everyone come and see them in a production.

A monologue tells a short story by a character in a play with a Point of Attack followed by a middle portion leading to a Climax, or at least the equivalent of a Curtain Line. It's the Climax or Curtain Line of the monologue that catapults us into the next scene or the resumption of dialogue.

Think of the monologue as a time when the emotion and complexity of a character's Subtext becomes overwhelming, a monologue is a great solution. And it tells a story -- either of an event that happened or an emotional development. Ideally, it does both of these at the same time.

In the good old days, playwrights had characters speak in paragraphs so the transition from dialogue to monologue was not an earth-shaking event. Now, with characters often only speaking in short phrases, the monologue is a very big deal, especially because there are usually only one or two monologues in a contemporary play. (Photo: Brenda Williams performs in the "NYC Deaf Fest" photographer: Don Petite Homme)

Vocabulary to master:
The Point of Attack is that first thing the audience will see or hear as the play begins. And it's one of the few decisions you face in this business that can make or break a great idea for a play. As an actor it is your entrance and first line – where did you come from, why did you enter? What is your goal?

Climax is the action or turning point, generally in a monologue this is when a character has been emotionally pushed to the point or revealing a secret, standing up for themselves, telling someone what they think of them or a very highly emotionally charged moment

A Curtain line is the same as an exit line or a punch line a lasting thought with impact on the audience. This term can also be used to describe where the curtain falls on the set when it is closed.

Subtext is the unspoken thoughts and motives of your characters -- what they really think and believe. We have all been in the situation when we were mad but it would be inappropriate to express it right then, or suspected someone of lying but had no proof and so kept our suspicions to ourselves. Another example would be unrequited love or hiding something that is for the other person's benefit.

Photo left: Eddie Swayze performs at NYC "Deaf Fest" photographer: Don Petit-Homme

In well-written dialogue, Subtext seldom breaks through the surface of the dialogue except in moments of extreme conflict. At other times, it colors the dialogue.

Subtext is what you think or feel underneath the Spoken Dialogue

Subtext is where the performers have room to create and interpret the role. If you let your characters tell each other everything they think or feel, actors can't do what they're trained to do best: revealing through gesture, intonation, and expression, the real essence of a character. Another aspect of subtext is the idea of "vocal music" (not necessarily spoken!) these are the "oh, ah, Lo, grrr, hmmm, huh, umm" additions to lines that are not written in. Actors need to make the lines feel spontaneous and "in the moment", in order to do that you can't always speak as if you know what you plan to say at every moment. Sometimes the emotional exclamation provides the energy to speak, other times you need to appear to search for the right word – there are an unlimited number of ways that the space between the lines can be filled with character and emotion.

Steps to working on a Monologue:

1. read it – it may seem obvious but many people impatiently jump to cold reading speaking it out loud or working on memorization. Restrain yourself! Read the monologue 2, 3 maybe 4 times.
2. Decide on who the character is talking to (even if they are not present on stage). Even people who seem to be talking to themselves may be talking to God, directly to the audience or practicing to talk with another character later in the play – like you would practice your answers in a job interview.
3. Weird word choices or phrases are clues. Look up anything that strikes you as odd, look on the internet or ask people. Be sure you understand the monologue
4. Research the play and playwright. What is the story that this monologue fits into, where does it appear in the play. Who wrote it and what do you think is the author's message

5. Who is this person? Do you know anyone remotely like them – same age, same body type, same job, something similar in the background – now do a cold reading as this person you think is similar to the character
6. How would you react if you were in the same situation as the character? If you would behave differently what would make you have similar emotions – give yourself the image or the fiction you need to sympathize with your character and see where they are "coming from"
7. Recite the monologue to yourself, using different emphasis and different subtexts.
8. Memorize the monologue – helpful ways to do this are to record (audio, video phone or web cam) yourself and play it to yourself while you are waiting on line, walking across campus. Also give yourself some movement that will help you remember what comes next (when I stand up I am talking about…when I move toward the audience I am talk about…) another way is to take the monologue line by line. Cover the line and say it, then look at the script to see if you were right or if you skipped something.
9. show it to someone – a roommate, a relative, a pet dog – notice what gets a reaction, a laugh, a nod, a smile, a frown – if its in the right places remember what you did, if its in the wrong places change that part of the monologue.

TRANSLATION – a unique process for Deaf actors

Since most of the productions that actors work on are published plays, printed in English this often puts the Deaf actor in the position of writing his or her own lines translating from English into American Sign Language (ASL). Even Deaf playwrights publish in English, so unless it is an original stage production written in ASL, it's highly likely that you will need some skills at creating an appropriate translation.

Most productions will offer the support of a Sign Coach, many even have a person who watches the translation to check for clarity and correct interpretation. But there are still those (especially if you are one of only a few Deaf actors in the cast) who will expect the Deaf actor to translate, interpret the role and memorize their own lines in the same amount of time they give to hearing actors who do not need to re-write the play.

Basic play analysis skills are helpful as well as some techniques for creating signs that are more reflective of your character's background than your own natural sign "accent". Begin by understanding the entire storyline – not just your role. Feel free to do research, watch a movie version, ask a friend - this is not cheating, it's research and is a valuable way in to the story in the shortest amount of time. Once you feel comfortable with the story break it down into its essential elements. Remember you do not want to translate word for word, you want to translate concept to concept. What follows are different ways of being sure you know what you are saying so that when you express it, you stay true to the playwright's intension and communicate character and information clearly enough for an audience to be comfortable understanding you.

ANALYSIS OF PLOTLINE

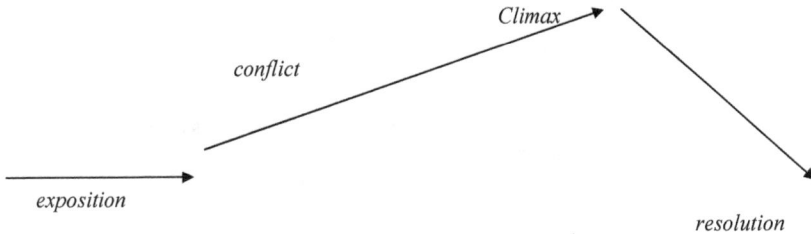

Climax

conflict

exposition

resolution

In order to summarize the story's plotline it is easiest to break the story down into its four essential elements, this helps you place the scenes you are in within the proper listener portion of the plot line. This can also help you to get a clear "shapshot" of the story without getting stuck in the details.

Character
protagonist:
This is not simply the "good guy" this character is the most important character in the story. If the story is told from his/her point of view or centers around their troubles they are the protagonist - even if they are Satan! Your character will have SOME opinion about this guy/girl.

antagonist:
This is not simply the "bad guy". This is the character who is the biggest obstacle to the main character or protagonist. Again your character will have an opinion about this character.

supporting characters:
These are the best friends or smaller characters in the story. They are called support because they backup either the protagonist or antagonist.

minor characters:
These are people who could be cut out of the story without losing any of the plotline.

No matter what function your character serves (how big or small the role) you want to create a fully developed person with a background and an opinion about what happens in the play. As you start to see your character in relationship to the plot and the other characters you need to be able to give more than just a physical description (no doubt they look a little like YOU!). What kind of people are they? You can draw conclusions about them by analyzing:

- what they do
- what they say
- what is said about them by others

You may also notice that some characters are unusual. They could be used by the author as:

- symbolic: they represent something other than simply themselves as a person
- satirical: they are used to comment on culture in a humorous way
- stock: expected types like lovers, villains, heroes, jesters
- realistic: almost as though you stepped into a real life
- exaggerated: extreme characters (like James Carey in THE MASK)

Setting

This is the location of the story. What era or time frame does it happen in? Place like a city? underwater? in a living room? In order to know if this is an important element in the story ask yourself:

- is the setting important to the plot?
- How would the story change if the setting were different?
- Setting includes, time, place and details of any surroundings.
- It gives the character an environment: weather can often set the mood for example.

CHARACTER TYPES

There is a visceral reaction to physicality that an audience feels immediately upon your first entrance, similar to visceral impressions of character, age and size that are followed in opera or musicals, plays too have stock characters. For example, you are already familiar with the commedia stock characters in which, sopranos are the love interest, tenors are romantic leads, altos are usually supporting roles, mezzos are villainesses or mothers, bass voices are villains or fathers. Your physicality dictates the sort of roles you will immediately be seen as fitting. Once a director has worked with you and knows your abilities more deeply you may be given an opportunity to explore more variety.

Class monologues: Tanya Yu, Ebony Williams, Zuleya Delgado, photographer; Luane Davis Haggerty

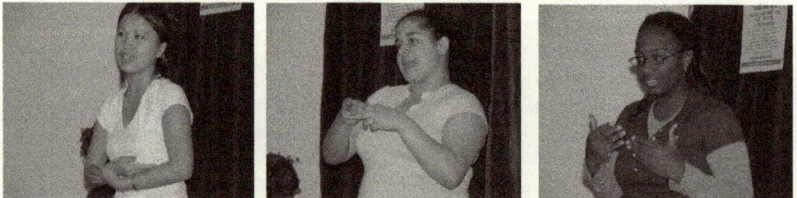

Character traits and styles - Baseline table:

Male 20-25 (generally ages to leading man)	Tall and fit	Conventionally Good looking	Sign Style- fluid/poetic Voice- Baritone or tenor	Romantic lead protagonist
Female 20-25 (generally ages to leading lady)	Short to average - fit	Conventionally Good looking (often blonde)	Sign- fluid/poetic Soprano or high alto	Ingénue protagonist
Male 20-25 (generally ages to character types – Dad, power-figure, working stiff, professor, lawyer, etc	Quirky look Very short/tall Very thin/heavy	Attractive in an off-beat way	Sign – accented, regional choices Unusual voice - "character" maybe a strong falsetto or very deep bass	Supporting roles – Best friend or Villains side kick (often comedic)
Female 20-25 (generally ages to character – mother,boss,off-beat waitresses,counselors etc.	Perky/cute Very short/tall Very thin/ heavy	Attractive in a Non-model-ish way (often brunette)	Sign – uses idiosyncrasies Unusual voice - "character" maybe a child-like sound or very sexy	Supporting roles- Best friend or Temptress Nosey neighbor etc. (often comic)
Male 20-25 (generally ages to leading man or villain)	Striking looking	Extremely handsome or off-putting/intimidating	Sign – strong, blades/fists Voice - deep or "character" Darth Vader – Ted Bundy	Antagonist villian
Female 20-25 (generally ages to leading lady or villainess)	Striking looking	Extremely beautiful or off-putting/intimidating	Sign – strong blades/fists Voice-mezzo	Antagonist

Do any of the "types" in the chart remotely fit your physical affect? Check off the elements that could match yours.

Special note – do not rate these types – one is not better than another all are crucial to the telling of the story and fighting against your type can be very self-defeating. Solos or more stage time doesn't make you more memorable – strong presence and skill do that.

Once you know who you are and what the story is there are several approaches to choosing your Sign expression.

Handshape:
- Conscious use of handshapes is often found in poetry, storytelling and percussion (or rhythmic) signing. Using ABC stories or communicating all with one handshape is useful for stylized characters (animals, characters who seem to speak in verse often)

- "soft" hand configurations (like "5", "C", "B") are relaxed an open, these are good choices for characters who are emotional or are love interests.
- "hard" hand configurations ("S", clawed "5") are tense choices good for villains or characters under stress.
- Detailed signs (or English initialized choices) are good for characters who imagine themselves to be intellectual
- Blades/fists are good sign choices for characters who are very physical

Movement:
- Keeping the movement path of signs consistent is pleasing and also makes it easier on the eye for reception. The movement path describes the physical details of the path of movement in a sign such as contact (VEHICLE-PARK), straight (STRAIGHT), circling (ALWAYS), zigzagging (VARIOUS) oscillating (CHILDREN), and bouncing (IMPROVE-GRADUALLY).
- "Tone" is the emotional underpinning of the line (not just a voice thing!). "Tones" of movement include: stretched, shortened, accelerated, slow motion, exaggerated, tensed, sharp staccato or fluid.
- Rate of motion is to sign fast, slow, jolting, dancingly, giddily as so on. Specifics about your character's background, intelligence and class can be used as suggestions for rate of sign choices.

Space/Location:
- On stage, it is helpful to match the special references of nouns to the blocking used in the play. For example, If Character X has a favorite chair that s/he sits in often maybe when you refer to that character you can point to the chair.
- Zone – if you are in a small intimate theater your sign zone may be similar to natural everyday spacing, if you are on a large stage your zone will need to expand to insure that the audience members sitting in the last row can see your signs as well as those in the front row. In spoken theater this is equivalent to elocution and diction.

Non-Manual Signals:
- This is the "vocal music" I mentioned before. Specific ASL examples of this are eyebrow shift, eye gaze, mouth movement, head nod, body shift.

Eye Contact:
- Eye contact implies a relationship with the audience.
- Use your gaze intentionally to guide the audience's eyes to the next line, show relationship to other characters on stage, show subtext.

Rhythm:
- Movement repetitions can be a fun way to show an eccentric character. It imposes on a line a regular reoccurrence of movements – sometimes one time, sometimes two times – seldom more than four times) the idea is to parcel the line into equal divisions of time.

- Pauses are very important do not be afraid of "silence" (the opposite of movement) sometimes a slight hold between lines or a hold for reaction or to let significance of information sink in are very useful.

A Monologue is one key tool a professional actor always has ready. The other is a photo/resume.
The sooner you begin to have one prepared the sooner you can begin to function as a working and professional actor. Most professional auditions will require you to bring a photo/resume with you and leave it with the director. Here is a description of what you need to prepare. I will expect that you have a photo/resume by the end of this course.

ACTING RESUME
What is an Acting Resume ?

Acting Resume - An actor's resume should list his physical description (height, hair color, eye color...), his credits (projects he has done), his contact info (usually the agent or manager), and his skills (sports, languages, hobbies). This information helps the theater director remember you after you have auditioned, so it's very important that it be accurate and reflect reality not fantasy! Your photo/resume can also be used as a first introduction. Once again you want to stand out but you want to be sure that if your photo/resume makes them call you, that you are who they expect to see when you finally meet. This in NOT like an on-line profile - lying is not acceptable.

Resume Dos and Don'ts

DO

☐ Print, glue or staple your resume to the back of your headshot.
☐ If you are stapling, trim your resume to fit the headshot. Cut your resume - 8x10.
☐ Make sure the contact information on the back is up-to-date, and that you have an email address.
☐ If you have a lot of projects, it's better to list the best ones first and not to worry if it is chronological order (in fact there is no need to add dates and years of production).

DON'T

☐ Never lie about your experience. The theater community is small and your lie will end up causing you embarrassment – someone will know!
☐ Don't make up special skills or write things down just to fill in the special skill area.
☐ Don't use a resume that is larger than 8 ½ x 11.
☐ Don't use a resume that is more than one page.
☐ Don't staple reviews or clippings to your resume. They just get in the way.
☐ Don't make the type smaller than 10 pt. If you have that much experience, edit it down.

Photo: Hilda Kasher and Stephanie Leyser audition for RIT Women's Center production of Vagina Monologues. Photographer: Luane Davis Haggerty

Acting Resume Sample

Here is an example of a real College student resume.

On the next page is just a sample resume and can be customized for your level of experience. If you don't have any experience, be sure to begin a resume with your contact information, then skills and any other useful information. If your character has a name, it is always better to put its name instead of the credit (Co star, featured, etc).

Martina Bell

Contact Information:
    e-mail: mnb1225@rit.edu
    Address : 1116 East 45th Street
    Chicago, IL 60653

eyes : Brown
hair: brown
height: 5'3"
weight: 100

Ethnicity : Black/African-American   Deaf – fluent in American Sign Language

Television experience
Law & Order Criminal Intent   featured extra   Universal Studios Inc
SAG Waiver "The Silencer"

Theatrical experience:
A Raisin in the Sun   Beneatha   NYC Deaf Theater
Festival
A Raisin in the Sun   Swing   NTID 1510 Theater
Lab
Lysistrata   Greek Chorus   NTID Panara Theater
Little Women   Jo March   NTID 1510 Theater Lab
Anne of Green Gables   Anne   Chicago Players
Night of the Living Dead   Chorus   Chicago Players
Deaf Jam Poetry   featured Poet   Dyer Art Gallery
The Tempest   Miranda   NTID Drama Club

Training
Acting: Method/Del-Sign Mary Vreeland, Luane Davis Haggerty
Stage Combat   Kelly Morgan
Translation for Stage   Patrick Graybill

YOUR NAME

Height: 5' 10"		Deaf – fluent American Sign Language
Weight: 160 lbs.		8686 Any Road
Hair: Black		Rochester, NY 14586
Eyes: Blue	E-mail	pager: 760-599-5400

Film/Television

Titanic	Mike	20th Century Fox
Over the Hedge	Supporting	DreamWorks
Star Wars	Featured	Lucas Films
Hart's War	Lead	MGM

Dance/Poetry/Storytelling

Lost	Guest Star	DeafJam
Jew Tales	Co Star	Grind Coffee House
Alias	Mr., Kahn	Community Theater

Theatre

Catch that man	Lou	Theatre of the Arts
Mental case	Bob	Elite Theatre
Lovely Tom	Tom	The Clash Theatre

Commercials

Nike	Athlete	B.B. Productions
Ford	Narrator	Mobile Video Productions

Training

Dan Sam	Stage and Screen	Los Angeles, California
Bobby Rid	Auditions Techniques	New York, New York

Specials Skills

Basketball, African Dancing, Martial Arts, Mime, Extreme Biking, Rock Climbing, Hip Hop, Singing, Stunts, Basketball, Football, Diving

HEADSHOTS

What are Headshots ?

Headshots – are an 8 x 10 sized photo of an actor's face. This is used in order to submit the actor through the mail for a specific role. It is also used during auditions to remind the director of who you are and what you look like after you have gone. Up until recently, the proper photo was in black and white. Today the photo can be a color one, and in some cases shows more than the actor's face. Some headshots shows 3/4 body shots, and there are some that show full body shots. But research shows that for best results, the clearer the face and the eyes are, the more you are likely to be called to an audition.

SAMPLE HEADSHOTS

Photos: In this chapter actors names are as printed – photographer Mark Benjamin

Headshots Tips !

Casting Director Diane Heery - Heery Casting Philadelphia

The headshot should LOOK LIKE YOU! It sounds simple, but too many shots come in that are "glamourized" or are 10 years old. Even if people say that your shot still looks good, if it's 5 years old- it's time for new pictures. 3/4, landscape or "head" shot are all good; this allows a little freedom for the actor's own "creativity" with their shot. If it's a little too artsy, it will detract from you and draw our attention to the "Art" of the shot. Color pictures seem to becoming the new trend - the ones that I've seen are very striking. Getting in for an audition depends more on your TALENT than your picture. The picture is just your introduction to casting directors and agents. Sometimes, but not often, an actor may be booked without auditioning, but that would only happen if we could guarantee that the actor in the picture is the actor that will show up for the booking! Most times, only extras are booked from headshots.

Casting Director John Strawbridge - Pat Moran & Associates Baltimore

There's no question that the most important thing about a headshot is that it look like you. You want to be sure you're called in for roles you're appropriate for, and not for roles you have no chance of getting. That's not something I "look for" - if I don't know you I can't judge that. If I do know you, then a headshot is really just a reminder, and the quality and style are much less important.

What I do look for in a headshot is a sense of who the actor is. I call a headshot the 1/125th of a second Audition. I look at the eyes. Do they project personality, confidence, and intelligence? Or do they say "Hurry up and take the picture!" I tend to prefer the 3/4 shots, since they give me a better sense of who the person is and what they look like. But, obviously, most of my work is with standard headshots, and that's fine. I don't care for color shots. They never look quite true. "Artsy" shots are fine... as long as I can still see what you look like, and that artsy is the personality you want to market.

Irma Girón

For example: Irma's headshot

The impression is that she is funny, quirky and comic. She is friendly and can do comedy. This is a great headshot to use for auditions that call for a comic character woman – a sidekick to the lead role.

If you look at Irma's features you can see that she could have done a more serious expression and made herself up glamorously. However, most of the roles she has been cast in are not that type of character and the competition for that type of character is often "model beautiful" she just wouldn't get as much work with a picture that is "pretty". This photo which really sells her personality more than her beauty is more useful.

For Example Jerald's headshot

Gerald is a dancer who is still working on his acting skills. What he will get most work in right now is dance and modeling. So he chose to go with a ¾ shot to emphasize his body and physicality.

He is presenting a friendly but neutral look which gives more flexibility. He could go tough guy character or leading man. The danger with staying neutral is you may not stand out or look "different" enough to catch a casting director's eye with just your picture. This photo works best when he has been seen in person at an audition, not just mailed his photo in for a call.

Jerald Greer
new york theatre agency 212.555.7060

Keo Phouminh

JULIAN IVANAVKA

The headshots on your left are "risky" or "arty" they are beautiful photos but they have no eye contact. Julian's headshot is "glamorous" and since the work he wants is as a model this can work for him – it won't get him many acting jobs. Keo is a hip hop dancer and choreographer; this thoughtful and "quirky" style will help emphasize that skill.

Joán Joel Campos

These actors can be more risky since they have representation by an agent who can work with them more, sell them to the directors and can target auditions for them. I'll discuss more about agents and managers later.

Joan's headshot would be more commercial if he had his eyes open and looking at the camera. This shot will be useful for dance auditions related to commercial work. It won't help him get an acting job

Compare the "risky" headshots (above) to the more traditional shots below. You can see how a clear expression and direct eye contact with the camera makes you feel like you have more communication with the actors in the traditional shots than you do with the actors in the arty shots.

Omobowaie Ayorinde

Christina Marie Cogswell

Kevin Nolan

Derrick Williams III

Activity– prepare your own resume, type up all of the performance work you can think of – poetry shows, school recitals, dance shows, use the guideline I provided.

Prepare your own theatrical headshot – a professional photo shoot can cost a great deal. If you are able to obtain a headshot from doing a performance, or if you have a friend who is a photographer value that resource! Be sure to thank those who help you create these materials. You will also want to make sure you have the ability to make copies of the image yourself. An active actor auditions up to 3 times every day.

Example of both resume and photo:

Troy Chapman

Troy Chapman

Contact Information:
e-mail roadrunner135@hotmail.com
3390 Dewberry Lane
Macedon, NY 14502
Height: 5'6"
Weight: 170lbs

ethnicity: African American
specialty – Hard-of-Hearing
voice and American Sign Language
Hair & Eyes: Brown

New York City Theater

Raisin In the Sun	Walter Lee Younger	NYC Deaf Theater Fest (IRT)
Windows Of the Soul	Lamar	NYC Deaf Theater Fest (IRT)
		Candidate for Pulitzer Prize
Emperor Jones	Brutus Jones	New 42nd Street Theater
		Winner OOBR Award
Tempest	Alonso	Quintero Theater
Walls (Remembering 9/11)	Karriefth	West Side Dance Project

Regional Theater

How to Succeed in Business		featured Chorus	Pittsford Musicals
West Side Story		Shark member	Panara theater
Laramie Project	Priest, DJ, reporter, Narrator	NTID PA Department	
12 Angry Men		Businessman	1510 Theater Lab
Boys Next Door		Counselor Jack	Panara Theater
Grinch Who Stole Christmas		Max	Panara Theater
Carmen		Lt. Andre	Dyer Art Gallery
Lobby Hero		Jeff	1510 Theater Lab
Soldier's Play		Peterson	1510 Theater Lab
Walls (Remembering 9/11)		Karriefth	tour

Dance Theater

Dance Train	Swing Dancer	PeaceArt Dance Co.
Vision Quest	character dancer	NTID/RIT Dance Company
Peter and the Wolf	forest Dancer	Thomas Warfield & Co.

ASL
Poetry

Deaf Jam Poetry	featured Poet	Dyer Art Gallery
Off the Page and On to Our Hands	Poet	Wallace Library
Read Our Lips	Poet	Grind Café

Training
Acting (Method) Mary Vreeland, (Del-Sign) Luane Davis Haggerty
Dance (Ballet, Modern, Jazz, African, ballroom) Thomas Warfield
Translation for Stage (ASL) Patrick Graybill
Special Skills – athletic all sports, basketball, pool, baseball, tennis, swim, track and field, driver's license and car, juggle (3 balls)

Homework #4

Pick and memorize a monologue

What follows are several Shakespearian monologues – each is printed as it appears in the script I have left room on the right side of the page for you to write in your own translation or "gloss" So as you look at it you will see that in the column on the left is the original English and what appears on the right is your handwritten ASL gloss. A gloss is a broken English representation of the ASL sign choices. It does not give references or location of signs, it does not take into account your personal sign style or that style of the character as you will decide to interpret that character. But the gloss should help you begin the translation process of turning your English monologue into a monologue able to be performed in Sign Language. Please don't feel that you must use the gloss completely – you have the freedom to make changes. But please do not think that means that you are able to paraphrase or to only perform the monologue in part. You still need to respect the playwright's work and do your best to perform the text as it was intended when written.

After you have 1) read the monologue 2) written your translation of what you think it means on the right side of the page 3) Answered the questions I have left for you to think about character. Begin the process of memorizing it. 1) Think of how you could say this in your own words, then add in the proper published words by repetition (video tape yourself and watch it often, have a friend watch and correct you. 2) Try to say the monologue 10 times daily to get comfortable with it.) 3) be ready to sign the monologue in class.

Above -Empty 1510-Theater Lab stage at NTID ready for you to state your monologue!
(photo Luane Haggerty)

HERE ARE YOUR CHOICES – PICK ONE OF THESE AND PREPARE FOR CLASS

Macbeth: 1.7.39-49

HERE IS THE MONOLOGUE IN ENGLISH WRITE YOUR TRANSLATION HERE

LADY MACBETH: Was the hope drunk

Wherein you dressed yourself? Hath it slept since?

And wakes it now, to look so green and pale

At what it did so freely? From this time

Such I account thy love. Art thou afeard

To be the same in thine own act and valor

As thou art in desire? Wouldst thou have that

Which thou esteem'st the ornament of life

And live a coward in thine own esteem,

Letting "I dare not" wait upon "I would,"

Like the poor cat i' th' adage?

What does this character want?	
Try to say the same thing in your own words.	
Try to do this monologue without any words at all – do it physically	
Who is this person talking to?	
Find any words that are repeated – use that handshape to sign this monologue (as much as you can) all in one handshape	

HERE IS THE MONOLOGUE IN ENGLISH WRITE YOUR TRANSLATION HERE

Richard III, 1.2.51-71

LADY ANNE: Foul devil, for God's sake, hence, and trouble us not,

For thou hast made the happy earth thy hell,

Filled it with cursing cries and deep exclaims.

If thou delight to view thy heinous deeds,

Behold this pattern of thy butcheries.

O, gentlemen, see, see dead Henry's wounds

Open their congealed mouths and bleed afresh! -

Blush, blush, thou lump of foul deformity,

For 'tis thy presence that exhales this blood

From cold and empty veins, where no blood dwells.

Thy deeds, inhuman and unnatural,

Provokes this deluge most unnatural-

O God, which this blood mad'st, revenge his death!

O earth, which this blood drink'st, revenge his death!

Either heaven with lightning strike the murderer

dead,

Or earth, gape open wide and eat him quick,

As thou dost swallow up this good king's blood

Which his hell-governed arm hath butchered.

Who is she talking to?	
What is her location?	

What is the word most repeated?	
Say this monologue in your own words	
Sign this monologue using only the "5" handshape (Blood, death, open, swallow etc.)	

HERE IS THE MONOLOGUE IN ENGLISH WRITE YOUR TRANSLATION HERE

The Tempest, 1.2.269-80

ARIEL: Safely in harbor

Is the King's ship. In the deep nook, where once

Thou called'st me up at midnight to fetch dew

From the still-vexed Bermoothes, there she's hid;

The mariners all under hatches stowed,

Who, with a charm joined to their suffered labor,

I have left asleep. And for the rest o' th' fleet,

Which I dispersed, they all have met again

And are upon the Mediterranean flote,

Bound sadly home for Naples,

Supposing that they saw the King's ship wracked

And his great person perish.

This character is not human – how does this character move?	
What are the various emotions this character goes through – highlight the different emotions in different colors (use at least five colors)	
Who is this character talking to?	
Tell this story in your own words	
Do this monologue without words	

HERE IS THE MONOLOGUE IN ENGLISH WRITE YOUR TRANSLATION HERE

King Lear, 1.1.135-45

LEAR: Peace, Kent.

Come not between the dragon and his wrath.

I loved her most, and thought to set my rest

On her kind nursery. Hence and avoid my sight!-

So be my grave my peace, as here I give

Her father's heart from her- Call France. Who stirs?

Call Burgundy. Cornwall and Albany,

With my two daughters' dowers digest this third;

Let pride, which she calls plainness, marry her.

Where is this person?	
Who is he speaking to?	
Say this monologue in your own words.	
What happened just before he spoke to make him want to say this?	
What answer does he want?	

HERE IS THE MONOLOGUE IN ENGLISH WRITE YOUR TRANSLATION HERE

Much Ado About Nothing, 1.1.235-42

BENEDICK: That a woman conceived me, I thank her; that she brought me up, I likewise give her most humble thanks. But that I will have a recheat winded in my forehead or hang my bugle in an invisible baldrick, all women shall pardon me. Because I will not do them the wrong to mistrust any, I will do myself the right to trust none. And the fine is, for the which I may go the finer, I will live a bachelor.

Why doesn't he trust women?	
Who is he talking to?	
Where will he go after saying this?	
What happened just before to make him say this?	

HERE IS THE MONOLOGUE IN ENGLISH WRITE YOUR TRANSLATION HERE

The Taming of the Shrew 1.2.201-213

PETRUCHIO: Why came I hither but to that intent?

Think you a little din can daunt mine ears?

Have I not in my time heard lions roar?

Have I not heard the sea, puffed up with winds,

Rage like an angry boar chafèd with sweat?

Have I not heard great ordnance in the field,

And heaven's artillery thunder in the skies?

Have I not in a pitchèd battle heard

Loud 'larums, neighing steeds, and trumpets clang?

And do you tell me of a woman's tongue,

That gives not half so great a blow to hear

As will a chestnut in a farmer's fire?

Tush, tush, fear boys with bugs!

Say this monologue in your own words	
Have you ever bragged about your own experiences with women to your friends?	
What did his friends tell him to make him say these things?	
What is he going to do after he says this monologue?	

YOU HAVE THE CHOICE TO WRITE YOUR OWN MONOLOGUE AS WELL

Guidelines –

If you choose to write in English:

Think of the opening as "http" like the computer address! This should be no more than 300-350 words

H= Hook. Your first sentence should be something that draws the audience to you through shock, surprise, odd fact or a question

T= Transition. Next you want to lead the audience smoothly to your main point or theme so you will transition from your hook to place where you can comfortably lead them to....

T= Theme. This would be the comment that hopefully the audience will remember after you are done it can be something the character struggled with, something they learned from the experience they are about to tell, or a deeply held belief the character has.

P= plan of development. Now you are going to lead the audience into the story

Tell us a story of an experience. You need to start with an exposition (who, what, when, where) then a conflict or problem, there should be one exciting moment or climax and the resolution.

End the monologue with a "button" or final thought – usually centered on reinforcing your theme.

If you choose to write in ASL:

Tell a story from your life – like:

- ➤ the most embarrassing moment
- ➤ first time experience
- ➤ life changing moment.

Use storytelling techniques like:

Cinematic technique – start with a big picture then narrow to a close up (example: show the whole city then narrow to two people sitting on a park bench)

Personification – take on the characteristics of characters that normally wouldn't be human (toys, magical characters, animals etc.)

Role shifting – show the full physical characteristics of the people in your story – show how they stand and show different sign choices or "accents" for these people.

Document your writing by videotaping this monologue for future use.

CHAPTER FIVE: Psychological Approaches to Acting

Quotes about Method acting

1923 Konstantin Stanislavski:
"The goal is not really to feel or see or touch something – that is hallucination – but to remember the mood when doing that."

1933 Lee Strasberg:
"emotional-memory allows an actor to recreate an experience from the past that affected him strongly giving the actors a key to express genuine emotion.

1936 Konstantin Stanislavski:
" With faith in your physical actions you will feel emotions, Therefore if you cannot create a human spirit in your part of its own accord, create the physical being of your role."

1938 Michael Chekov:
"In refining the psychological gesture, the body is a means of finding a specific feeling."

1963 Grotowski:
"We do not possess memory, our entire body is memory."

1958 Sanford Meisner:
"Listen to your body you will find the character "actions" "intentions" and "objectives" arise organically within the work itself, without the actor needing to sit down and do "table work" to figure them out."

(Image on right from the movie "On the Waterfront" used with permission from 20th Century Pictures Archives)

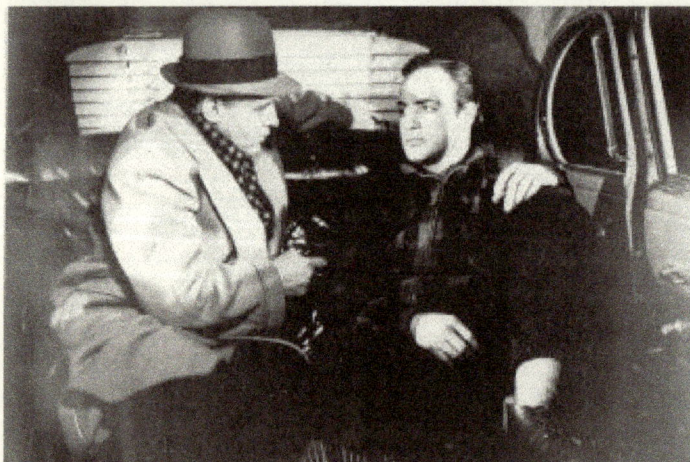

As acting styles entered the twentieth century most actors were well trained in the technical and physical aspects of acting, but it was the actors who were able to use those techniques in ways that were more emotional who became successful rather than those who turned technique into empty mechanical gestures. The goal became to keep the useful aspects of physicality that most actors were already familiar with and to add in an emotional and intellectual element that would help the actor to achieve a realistic portrayal of a character. The best known of these approaches to acting is called "The Method" and was first developed by the Russian director Konstantin Stanislavski.

The problem with present day "Method" actors is their lack on knowledge of the foundation and physical techniques that need to be in place before psychological work can begin. We are all raised watching television and movies with the small facial movements, minimal body language and subtleties that are needed for that medium and so many well-trained actors today are missing the physical base needed for live stage. To create a fully rounded character both the physical as well as the psychological are necessary.

The Method –Method acting is an acting technique in which actors try to replicate the emotional conditions under which the character operates in real life, in an effort to create a life-like, realistic performance. "The Method" typically refers to the generic practice of actors drawing on their own emotions, memories, and experiences to influence their portrayals of characters.

Origins

Group Theater in N.Y. City 1930s?
L-R. Roman Bohnen, Morris Carnovsky?, Unkwn
Phoebe Brand, Elia Kazan, Clifford Odets?, Lee J. Cobb

Mainly an American school, "The Method" was popularized by **Lee Strasberg** at The Actors Studio and the Group Theatre, in New York City in the 1940s and 1950s. It was derived from "the Stanislavski System", after **Konstantin Stanislavski,** who pioneered similar ideas in his quest for "theatrical truth." This was done through friendships with Russia's leading actors as well as his teachings, writings, and acting at the Moscow Art Theater (founded 1897).

Strasberg's students included quite a few of America's most famous actors of the 20th century, including Paul Newman, Al Pacino, James Dean and many others.

Technique

Some consider Method acting difficult to teach. Partially this is because of a common misconception that there is a single "method." "The Method" (versus "the method" with a lower-case m) usually refers to Lee Strasberg's teachings but really no one method has been laid down. Stanislavski himself changed his method constantly and dramatically over the course of his career. He used **Meyerhold's** system of biomechanics as the physical partner to his work. In general, method acting combines a careful consideration of the psychological motives of the character and some sort of personal identification with and possibly the reproduction of the character's emotional state in a realistic way. It usually forms an antithesis to clichéd, unrealistic, and so-called rubber-stamp or indicated acting. Mostly, however, the surmising done about the character and the elusive, capricious or sensitive nature of emotions combine to make method acting difficult to teach. In general, the approach with gifted actors is to simply introduce the technique and allow them to find their own "way in" through monologues, once they have found an individual approach and can "hold" their own stage scene work is begun.

Depending on the exact version taught by the numerous directors and teachers who claim to propagate the fundamentals of this technique, the process can include various ideologies and practices such as "as if", "substitution," "emotional memory" and "preparation".

Lee Strasberg (November 17, 1901 – February 17, 1982) was an American actor, director and acting teacher. He cofounded, with directors Harold Clurman and Cheryl Crawford, the Group Theatre in 1931, which was hailed as "America's first true theatrical collective". In 1951, he became director of the non-profit Actors Studio, in New York City, considered "the nation's most prestigious acting school". In 1969, Strasberg founded the Lee Strasberg Theatre and Film Institute in New York City and in Hollywood to teach the work he pioneered. He is considered the "father of **method acting** in America," according to author Mel Gussow, and from the 1920s until his death in 1982 "he revolutionized the art of acting by having a profound influence on performance in American theater and movies".[4] From his base in New York, he trained several generations of theatre and film's most illustrious talents, including Anne Bancroft, Dustin Hoffman, Montgomery Clift, Marlon Brando, James Dean, Marilyn Monroe, Julie Harris, Paul Newman, Al Pacino, and Robert De Niro. (**For more information see -** http://www.strasberg.com/lstfi/)

Sample Exercises: 1) Create a written biography for your character as a living breathing person. When were they born, where did they go to school, where do they live? What kind of family did they grow up in? 2) Find some experience from your own life that is similar to what happens to the character in the script. Tell your story as if the character were talking about you.

Sanford Meisner, another Group Theatre pioneer, championed a separate, though closely related, school of acting which came to be called the **Meisner technique.** Meisner broke from Strasberg on the subject of "sense memory" or "emotion memory", one of the basic tenets of the American Method at the time. Those trained by Strasberg often tried to experience all sensations as the character would and often used personal experience on stage to identify with the emotional life of the character and portray it. Meisner found that too cerebral and advocated fully immersing oneself in the moment of a character and gaining spontaneity through an understanding of the character's objectives and through exercises he designed to help the actor gain emotional investment in the scene and then free him or her to react as the character.

Sample Exercise: 1) Using a ball to represent energy; as you say your line in a scene throw the ball to the next person to speak. This will lead to proper eye contact, listening skills, and reacting to lines in addition to acting the line.

2) Using any found object in the room have each actor use that object in mime in different ways. This releases the individual from literal understanding of the world around you and develops a more improvisational approach.

Stella Adler, the coach whose fame was cemented by the success of her students Marlon Brando and Robert DeNiro, as well as the only teacher from the Group Theatre to have studied Acting Technique with Stanislavski himself, also broke with Strasberg and developed yet another form of acting. Her technique is founded in the idea that one must not use memories from their own past to conjure up emotion, but rather use circumstances from their imagination. She also emphasized, like Sanford Meisner, the all-importance of "action" within the theatre. As she often preached, we are what we do, not what we say.

Sample exercises –

- Use of memory – use your own personal memories of past hurts or joys and graft them onto the character you are playing, pull up those memories when your character needs to display emotional responses.
- Use music to evoke emotion, either during the development process or as you prepare to perform.

Uta Hagan (12 June 1919 – 14 January 2004) was a German-born American actress. She originated the role of Martha in the 1963 Broadway premiere of *Who's Afraid of Virginia Woolf* by Edward Albee (who called her "a profoundly truthful actress"). Hagen was on the Hollywood blacklist, in part because of her association with Paul Robeson, and this curtailed film opportunities, focusing her to perform in New York theaters. She won the Tony Award three times. She later became a highly influential acting teacher at New York's Herbert Berghof Studio and authored best-selling acting texts, *Respect for Acting* and *A Challenge for the Actor*. She was elected to the American Theatre Hall of Fame in 1981.[1]

Sample Exercises – You are asked to find a character very different from yourself – a magical character (elf, ghost, witch etc.) and an animal character. In class imagine how these three characters move, gesture and speak. Improvise a short monologue about something in their life that is causing them trouble.

Michale Chekhov (29 August 1891 – 30 September 1955) Chekhov was considered by the Russian theatre practitioner Constantin Stanislavski to be one of his brightest students. He studied under Stanislavski at the First Studio of the Moscow Art Theatre, where he acted, directed, and studied Stanislavski's 'system'. He later led the company of the studio under the name the Second Moscow Art Theatre. Stanislavski came to regard Chekhov's work as a betrayal of his principles. But actor's who studied under Checkov found his approach to be very useful and it became a respected school of study in the American Theater professional community.

Sample exercises: Chekhov taught a range of movement dynamics such as molding, floating, flying, and radiating that actors use to find the physical core of a character. His techniques, though seemingly external, were meant to lead the actor to a rich internal life. For our purposes a sample of movement dynamics would be – a game of statues. Have the actors move freely and then shut out the lights. They actors should freeze in whatever position they were in when the lights went out. When the lights come back up have then define what they are doing, what their character is thinking and feeling and improvise a monologue that begins with them in the frozen position.

TO READ MORE –

- *Respect for Acting* by Uta Hagen
- *An Actor Prepares* by Konstantin Stanislavski
- *To the Actor* by Michael Chekhov
- *Sanford Meisner on Acting* by Sanford Meisner
- *Method or Madness* by Robert Lewis
- *Advice to the Players* by Robert Lewis
- *Slings and Arrows: Theater in My Life* by Robert Lewis
- *The Actor's Studio: A Player's Place* by David Garfield
- *Miranda is Beautiul: A Biography* by Miranda Vittoria Graham

Top -Lee Strasberg, Stanislavsky, Bottom - Sandford Meisner and Uta Hagan
Photos from Lincoln Center for the Performing Arts Archives public domain.

Constantin Stanislavski
(1863-1938)

Character Analysis
pick a character from a comic strip or use the comic printed here

the audition   Luane Haggerty

the list of winners

I hope I get in

SHe always gets picked I don't know why she's worrying!

Hey who knew they only wanted guys! Heck! I didn't even try!

I feel bad for the girls

This comic strip was created at MakeBeliefsComix.com. Go there to make one yourself!

Type out your answers on a separate sheet of paper
Method Acting (Lee Strasberg based on Stanislavski) When writing out your answers do not indulge in "I don't know" or "I guess" you get to decide these answers as you create this character so make some decisions.

How old is your character?

Male or female?

What kind of education have they had?

Explain how your answers fit the information you have in the comic:

What family relationships does your character have?
Mother?
Father?
Brother?
Sister?
Cousins?

What relationships does you character have in the specific comic you are looking at?

Are there any possible romantic relationships for your character?

Who are your friends?

Who are your enemies?

List all of the other characters in your comic and explain who they are related to YOUR character:
1)
2)
3)
4)

Describe how this character is like you.

Family?

Other relationships?

age and body type?

Have you had experiences like what you character has to go through?

Did you handle yourself the same way or differently?

Describe in detail the story of your real life experience that is comparable to the story of what the character goes through.

Psychological Acting Homework
"My Front Porch"

1) Observe the people around you. Try to identify people you haven't noticed before
   – maybe someone who lives in your dorm
   - Maybe a janitor or cleaning person
   - Maybe someone who is eating at the dinning commons

What makes them different from the people you normally hang out with? Age? Clothes?
Different schedule? Different location for classes and living?

2) Pick one person and take their photograph (your should probably even ask them
   so you don't appear to be a stalker!)
3) Create a biography for them – it doesn't have to be true but try to base some of
   the information on things you can observe about them.

Biography:
Name:
Age:
Where did they grow up?
What kind of family did they have?
What were some of their proud moments?
What were some of their obstacles?
What kind of friends do they have?
Why did they come to Rochester?
What was their educational level?
What do they do here (job? Study?)?
What are their goals for the future?
What kind of family or relationships do they have now?

*some of these you need to make up completely others might be suggested by their
appearance. What kind of clothes are they wearing? Jewelry? how do they move? What
kind of food they do they eat? Who do you observe them talking to? Use what you
observe to help you create a character for this person.

PHOTO ANALYSIS FOR CHARACTER WORK –

Snap a photo of someone you see in your life daily, but it must be someone you don't really know very well. Then interview that person to find out more – what are some of the things you didn't know but make a change in how you see that person now.

Example –

My analysis is focused on the man in the middle right –
Name: Norm Grinder
He is 68 years old and grew up on a farm outside of Rochester. He is a very active happy person and had a big family. His parents are gone but he is still close to one sister. He has a job as a Mailman and misses the walking, so now he walks for exercise with a group of friends at breakfast time one day a week. He went to college and has traveled a lot. In the future he would like to meet a nice older woman and settle down. He lives in an apartment building and likes to go to book readings or music concerts.

I didn't know – He had marched with Martin Luther King Jr. in Selma Alabama. I had thought he had never lived outside of Rochester and so was more close-minded than he actually is.

Psychological Methods of Acting Quiz
Please type your answers on a separate sheet of paper

Match the quote

Grotowski ____

A) "The goal is not really to feel or see or touch something – that is hallucination – but to remember the mood when doing that."

Chekov _____

B) "emotional-memory allows an actor to recreate an experience from the past that affected him strongly giving the actors a key to express genuine emotion.

Strasberg _____

C) " With faith in your physical actions you will feel emotions, Therefore if you cannot create a human spirit in your part of its own accord, create the physical being of your role."

Stanislavski ____

D) "In refining the psychological gesture, the body is a means of finding a specific feeling."

Meisner _____

E) "We do not possess memory, our entire body is memory."

Adler _____

F) "Listen to your body you will find the character "actions" "intentions" and "objectives" arise organically within the work itself, without the actor needing to sit down and do "table work" to figure them out."

True or False
There is only one Method acting _____
Stanislavski didn't believe in physical techniques ____
Biomechanics finds emotion in the body ____
Lee Strasberg was Russian ____
Stanislavski created The Method _____
The Actors Studio and The Group Theater used psychological methods of acting ____
Stella Adler was the only method teacher to have studied with Stanislavski _____
The "Method" typically refers to the generic practice of actors drawing on their own emotions, memories, and experiences to influence their portrayals of characters._____
It is best to blend emotion, physical work and text when creating a character_____

CHAPTER SIX: Business of Theater

Although most beginning actors focus on the art or craft of theater it is important to keep an eye on the fact that it is a business. The Actor's Equity Association (AEA - the actor's union) notes that at the height of the employment season for actors (summer) there is still 80% unemployment for union members. Although this does not take into account the number of actors working for no pay or actors who have created their own work, it is a chilling statistic nonetheless.

It is this statistic that non-theater people draw on when they discourage friends or relatives from entering the theatrical industry. However, there are very many people (myself included) who have worked in theater non- stop nearly all their lives. How do they do it?

Photo: Dr. Simon Carmel talks with the cast of "Windows of the Soul" photographer – Julie Busch

Marketing yourself

"The soul desires to dwell in the body because without the members of the body it can neither act nor feel." – Leonado Da Vinci

Do not be tempted to drastically change yourself to match some "American Idol" ideal. Everything that makes you unique is what insures that you will be noticed and will stand out from the crowd at auditions. For example; several friends of mine; dyed hair, fixed teeth, got contacts, lost or gained weight in an attempt to look "commercial". What they succeeded in doing was to match the 100 other blonde blue-eyed skinny model-types going out for the same roles. They blended in and unless they already had incredible credits on their resume or had a startlingly different vocal, physical or acting approach they got lost in the shuffle.

When you ask people to name successful actors, many people list celebrities, particularly female celebrities who are all of a similar type. But when you really look for actors, you will notice that they are all very unique in some way. So if you are short, heavy-set, ethnic, very tall - rejoice that you are different from the crowd and you have the advantage of standing out. It's up to you to "sell" the fact that your physical type more clearly embodies the character than a more generic type. You also need to realize that there are many more people making their living as actors than just the few you see in newspapers, on CNN or in the movies. Many working actors never become famous – they just work consistently, earn a living wage, have health care, raise families, buy houses and other ordinary things. Because there is little written about these actors they become invisible to people who are not working in theater. But common sense will tell you, all those theaters producing shows all across the country are not all staffed with celebrities.

So how do you become a working actor? This requires you to do a little research before you go to an audition. Look up the play on the web, check out the cast list find a synopsis; you disempower yourself when you go in "blind". When you go to an audition, you decide what role you really want, choose material that supports the fact that you can do that character, and mention it when you are in the room with the director.

If you find you are often cast in roles of a similar type – make sure your photo resume reflects that (even if you are the "villain" and you wish you were the hero) so you can make it easier for the director to quickly identify where you fit into their cast. Dress in a way that makes your advantages clear. For example, are you "the secretary" then dress in business clothes, are you the "crazy neighbor" wear something colorful and artistic. The only caution is if you feel your best trait is physical attractiveness and you dress provocatively – you may get the wrong response.

Exercise: Identify your type. First, create your "dream" resume. What are the roles you hope to play? Can you notice a pattern? Next, ask a friend to list five TV actors who s/he thinks do the sort of roles you could do. Are the two lists complimentary or are they VERY different? If they are the same you probably already know and accept your "type, if they are very different, you need to do more reflection on the characters you would most likely be cast as easily.

Getting others to market you

Since many actors have difficulty doing both the business and the art there are managers and agents that can be hired in this industry. A manager typically has a small client base, they offer the actor an objective view and they have access to agents, casting directors and others who are able to hire you. Most managers receive no pay if you are not working, but when you do work they take between 10-15% of your paycheck.

Story – I had always wanted to do musical theater in the style of Fred and Ginger movies and so I found a partner and we put together an act. We interested a manager in helping us do cruise line and hotel work. After seeing us perform he pointed out that the bad news - we couldn't be Fred and Ginger, the good news was we could be brilliant as Luane and Jonathan. We couldn't see that distinction but once we made the changes he suggested we began to work regularly. He had earned the percentage since we wouldn't have made any of the money without him.

Another actor's advocate is an agent. Generally, they are more powerful and have many contacts. They are eligible for a service called "the breakdowns" which is sent on e-mail four times a day from Broadway producers, film directors, casting agents, commercial companies, industrial event organizations etc. Most of these types of work are very high paying. Although agents are basically employment agents, there are so many people in need of their services that they tend to pick and choose who they will help. Getting an agent to represent you can take a lot of focused energy. The use of a resource called *The Ross Reports* list them all with their addresses, who they like to represent and if they are willing to see new people. Once you get an agent you still need to stay in contact and remind them to work on your career, since they often have several hundred clients. They will take 25-35% of your paycheck.

Unions

Actors are often taken advantage of. We are trained to please and say "yes". In general, high school, college and Community Theater may ask inexperienced actors to work long hours, in potentially unsafe situations and may even ask the actors themselves to work on sets or costumes. This is not exploitive since the exchange is intensive experiential learning which prepares the actor for the rigors and endurance needed for paying work. The step into non-professional theater which pays the actor a fee and recognizes their growing skill is the place where most actors learn to assert their rights.

Story – Several actors were cast in New York to do summer stock in Florida. They paid their own way to the theater to find they would be sleeping in what had recently been horse stalls. When it rained snakes, frogs and other wild life appeared. When the actors protested asking for better housing the producer left with all of the money. They had no pay check or ticket home. Had they been union members they would have had an organization to complain to who would have offered assistance.

There is a catch-22 in joining the union. You must have a union contract before you can join, but you can't audition for union shows without a union card. So how does everyone get in? As you build your resume you will make contacts, sooner or later one of these contacts will direct or produce a union show and will cast you because they have worked with you before. Another way is to wait until the end of the union auditions and if time is left they will see a small number of non-union people (check out playbill on line or the tradepaper Backstage for those audition notices). It requires persistence and a high level of skill once you get in the room to audition.

Who are they?

AEA or Equity – (Actors Equity Association) The professional union for Stage Actors, covers Broadway, Regional, and summer stock contracts

AFTRA – (American Federation of television and Radio Artists) The professional union for DJs, Soap opera actors, television workers, commercial actors etc. This is one of the most powerful unions presently since they have a high percentage of working members.

SAG – (Screen Actors Guild) The professional union for movies and film work

AGVA – (American Guild of Variety Artists) nearly defunct union whose work is to protect novelty acts. They were very strong during vaudeville days and still cover performers in hotels, circus, and occasionally cruise line settings.

SSD&C – (Society of Stage Director and Choreographers) Only covers Directors and choreographers who work in college, Broadway, Regional, Industrial or other high paying situations. But they also help their members get this type of work through observerships and mentoring programs.

Photo: David Woolwrath and David Koran in a scene from "The Zoo Story"

7 Audition Must-Haves
Be sure to bring these 7 things to your next audition….

The character
The most important thing to bring to any audition is also the most overlooked. You must bring the character! Bring the character! Is the character shy? Then don't be loud and obnoxious at the audition. Is the character a bad boy? Then don't go to the audition in a shirt and tie. Be your character from the moment you walk in the door to the moment you leave and at all times in between. The more the casting directors can see you as the "shy guy" or "bad boy" or whatever the character is, the more likely you are to land the role.

Extra clothes
It is usually not necessary to bring another outfit. But what if you arrive at an audition

and discover that your desired character wears a tie? Having a tie in your car could give you a leg up. You run to the car, put it on, and look the part better than your competition.

Necessary accessories
Is the character a basketball player? Why not bring along a basketball to use with the audition? Is she a journalist? How about a notebook and a pair of glasses? Remember, you want the casting director to see you as the character they are looking for.

A watch

Why? So you can get there with time to spare. Being late is a killer. Plus, getting there early allows you to read over the script, prepare and maybe even make an early impression on the casting directors. It also helps keep your nervousness and stage fright under control.

Acting Script/Sides
If you are fortunate enough to get the script ahead of the audition, you are lucky. If it's a "cold" audition have all of your monologues with you so if they ask for a different choice in the moment you can look through what you know. Even if you have them all memorized it's still a good idea to bring them with you at the audition.

5 Headshots with Resume
The casting director will always need 1 or 2 to help make his final decision. Still, you should always have a few more, just in case one of the other project's managers or actors think you would be great for a part elsewhere. This is your "business card" in the industry you need to be sure it is of good quality, clear to read and represents your work well. A bad or unprofessional picture is nearly useless, an unorganized resume won't be read.

A warm smile and friendly personality

Why would they want to work with you otherwise? Also remember to be nice to everyone you meet – you never know when someone who seems to be "just another actor" is a friend of the director or when the audition monitor is actually a person on the production team.

"any business person who does not consider the customer the most important element in the enterprise, is doomed to failure. Becoming a successful performer is a matter of performing in front of an audience as much as you possibly can"

– Joseph Papp, NYC Public Theater

If You Want Work It's There To be Had – But YOU Have to go Get It

For those actors who really make all their money through theater work, creativity is an important element. Suppose you don't audition well or there are just not a lot of auditions for the type of performer you are. That doesn't mean there are not enough jobs to sustain a career. But it might mean you have to get creative to find them and get hired. The traditional "ladder" of going to auditions, getting hired and then getting an agent may not work for you. So what can you do? (Photo above Acting fall 2010 Class, photographer Lisanne Houkes)

Audition anyway! Be careful to enjoy the auditions and understand that the point may not be to get hired. The point may be just to practice auditioning so when that one big important audition comes along you are rehearsed and ready.

Audition anyway! So the Casting call didn't ask for a Deaf performer – if you show up and make an impression they may realize that making the character in the play Deaf would be a really good idea.

Audition anyway! What if there are no interpreters? Shouldn't the theater pay to have one ready to go just in case? In heaven all auditions would have a skilled pianist and an interpreter ready to support your audition. Unfortunately, in real life you may have to take care of this kind of support yourself. Many actors who sing pay a pianist to come to auditions with them so that they are confident that they can show their best vocal skills. You may find it a good idea to pay an interpreter to come with you for the same reason. Suppose you don't have the money? Deaf performers can call ahead and request an interpreter be at the audition, but as you know, even when requested sometimes there are no interpreters who take the job so you will be stuck auditioning at a "special" time instead of at the same time that the director is seriously casting the other roles.

Here's a little used possibility (that I have done for many friends and we have had success), a surprising number of interpreters like theater and would like to audition too. Many times if they go with you to the audition they get to be "seen" twice – once as an interpreter and once as an actor. Because of this it is possible to get them to attend the audition with you and interpret for free. This often results in getting BOTH of you cast since the director can see how easy it would be to work with you if a performance savvy interpreter is around too.

Audition anyway! What if there are just no auditions that are useful to go to? Why not put together your own show and use that opportunity to invite all of the theater contacts you have and all of the agents who handle Deaf performers to attend. When they come to see you, have your photo/resumes ready in a package for those who are interested in your talents to take with them. Keep a list of the people who came and stay in contact with them. No doubt the next time they have an audition for a role you would be right for, the will invite you to come. They may even be impressed enough with your performance to cast you in something just from watching you perform. In essence you just created your own "showcase" audition opportunity.

Suppose you audition but you are only offered roles in shows that do not pay you to act. Take the gig! It is better to be performing than it is waiting to perform. Each time you do a show; you add credits to your resume, learn new skills and meet new people. Those new people can help you get the next job. Not to mention you now have a time and place for agents to come see you perform. Watching you in action will always be more impressive than seeing you at an interview just talking.

There are more ways to make money with your skills – if you can get creative!

Suppose you have auditioned like crazy and no job has been offered. Try making your own show! If you have created your own show, you can contact schools, senior organizations, cultural organizations, libraries etc and sell them your show. Send them photos from the performance, describe the story, maybe even include some comments from the audience. Decide how much you need to make and how much the organization can afford to pay and you can work for YEARS making your living performing that way. If your show is flashy enough you might even be able to interest theaters, colleges, cruise lines and hotels into hiring you.
(photo right Zack Taylor Acting 2010 Class, photographer Luane Haggerty)

FIRST –

What is it makes makes you special? Are you funny, can you dance, roller skate, hip hop dance? Do you like puppets? Incredible costumes? Fabulous make-up? Other than the creation of a character, what do you do that gets attention? Let's suppose you can juggle.

Be sure to put that special skill on your resume – it is usually those skills that will get you in the door to get your first commercial work.

SECOND –

Who responds best to your special skill? Little kids? People your own age? Senior citizens? People who go clubbing? This is how you define your audience. If your skill is as a juggler you have already noticed that kids are easily amazed with what you do. If you can make up a routine that lasts between 30-50 minutes you need to think about selling your work to: birthday parties, elementary schools, after school programs, Gyms, churches, summer camps with programs for kids.

Figure out how much you need to make an hour (your time, gas to get there, costumes, equipment and rehearsal time can be figured in. You then make up a web page, a brochure, a business card and start letting people know. People will recommend you to other people and you will have plenty of work.

THIRD –

expand on that idea! Now that you have started getting people to call you asking to pay you to perform, you can grow your idea. Maybe you have a few friends that you LOVE performing with – create a show together and market that to better paying places, cruise ships, hotels, weddings, industrial shows, street fairs, County fairs etc.

The best part about creating your own work is you are in charge of your own schedule, so if you get an opportunity to be in a theatrical production you can turn down the smaller shows to make time for rehearsals and performances without "losing your job" the way actors who make their day job from something more removed like office work or waitering. Anytime they ask to leave for a show they risk losing their job. If you make your own work, you leave when you want and go right back to it when you have to.

(Photo left Wesley Weiss Acting 2010 Class, photographer Luane Haggerty)

Getting back to the more conventional forms of theater, finding jobs in productions can be tricky until you find out how the folks in your city or town advertise themselves. You may wonder where can you find ads for the auditions? In every city there will be a newspaper that carries audition notices. In Rochester the City News often lists auditions for local theater. Do a little research on the internet. There are many audition sites and many talent agencies you don't always have to be in a big city to find them – although big cities generally have more auditions (because they have more theaters).

Avoid any place that asks you to pay for access to the information. In general they are not really able to tell you about good places to work.

Here are some useful links to get you started:
www.Deafcasting.com

www.Playbill.com

Backstage tradepaper http://casting.backstage.com/

Actor's Equity Association
Homepage : http://www.actorsequity.org/CastingCall/castingcallhome.asp

Deaf Network of Texas http://deafnetwork.com/wordpress/blog/2010/01/11/deafia-auditions-rehearsal-schedule/
Deaf West Theater www.Deafwest.com
National Theater for the Deaf http://ntd.org/
New York Deaf Theater http://www.nydeaftheatre.org

http://www.redbirdstudio.com/AWOL/combaud.html REGIONAL COMBINED
AUDITIONS (February and March)
Drama Book Store - can order any script, score or publication on theater
http://nycstagecasting.blogspot.com/

Best publications: The Ross Report (monthly magazine that lists all of the agents in New York)
Backstage Newspaper – weekly newspaper that lists all of the auditions happening in New York that week.
FYI –
Dr. Haggerty's New York Company – Interborough Repertory Theater (IRT) Holds an annual Deaf Theater Festival and has a wing that is "ASL Creative"
http://irttheater.org/

Photo: Karriefth Norman and Troy Chapman with "sides (audition scripts) for roles in "Law & Order" photographer: Luane Davis Haggerty

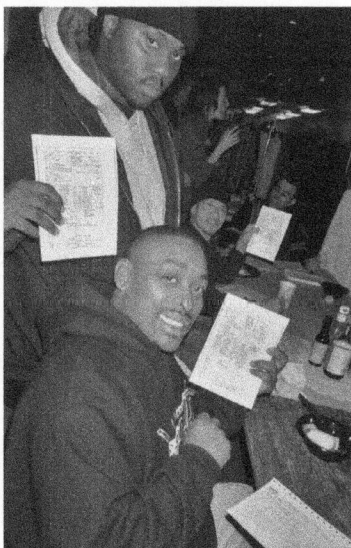

HOMEWORK #6

Prepare a photo/resume and a monologue to present in class this will be equal to your midterm exam. You may be asked to refine this presentation and use it as your final exam as well. It is worth your time to take this assignment seriously and do the best you can.

Checklist for a strong audition

Material
√ You have the type and length of material needed
√ You have material that you think is well-written and that you enjoy

Entrance
√ You have a confident, positive entrance & introduction and seem happy to be there
√ You have a clean transition from your introduction to beginning the piece

Directing Choices
√ You have identified a clear beginning, middle, climax, and end
√ You have clear staging that tells your story
√ You consistently perform your monologue at a comfortable distance from your auditors
√ Your monologue is physically specific and fun to perform
√ There is variety - the monologue doesn't stay on the same mood/tone

Acting Choices
√ You know exactly what your character wants from those he is speaking to
√ You have a simple, clear acting objective that you believe in and care about

Performance
√ You know your monologue and staging so well that you are free to play
√ Your voice is supported and expressive throughout
√ Every word is clearly articulated and easy to understand
√ You are easily seen throughout the monologue
√ You know your lines and staging cold - you can do them no matter what
√ It is clear what you want from the person/people you are talking to
√ You are pursuing your acting objective fully throughout the monologue
√ Your whole body is engaged in your performance
√ You have a strong, clear ending to your monologue
√ You have a clean transition to your 'thank you'

Exit
√ You have a confident, positive exit from your audition, OR
√ You are prepared to stay and chat if your auditors ask you to

Business of Theater Quiz

Performers unions –
What to the following theatrical unions' initials stand for and who do they protect?

AEA

AFTRA

SAG

AGVA

SSD&C

What is known as the actor's business card?_____
a) Monologues   2) audition appointment   3) photo/resume   4) agent

Which list of audition materials is most useful?____
   a) 4 monologues/2 songs b) a prepared programme c) 2 contrasting songs d)
   cold reading.

What is the best auditioning strategy?___
   a) go to every audition you can find b) go only to auditions for shows you can
   fit into your schedule c) go only to auditions for roles which are your "type"
   d) Do as many auditions as you can do and research the roles.

An agent will be most impressed with you if you.._____
   a) have a degree in theater b) have a lot of credits on your resume c) give a
   good interview d) can show them newspaper reviews of your work.

True or False:
It is more important to be a principal actor than be in the chorus _____
Building skills must happen before building a resume ____
Being a clear "type" will get you more work _____
Acting for TV, movies, and stage requires the same technique _____
Being versatile will give you a longer career _____
Producing your own work in theater is "vanity work" _____

CHAPTER SEVEN: Stage Combat

PHOTO: Acting Class at Roberts Wesleyan College Photographer: Luane Davis Haggerty

Despite the appearance of danger, stage combat has more in common with dance than violence. As you examine the standard plotlines of drama you will see that nearly every play will have a climactic scene in the second act which usually contains a chase or a fight of some sort. In order to protect the actor's safety and to insure that the show can run for more than one performance (!) it is crucial that any physical movement on stage that can cause personal harm be taken seriously and focused attention on three elements should occur; 1) equipment, 2) choreography, 3) repetition.

Equipment
Guns – Many low budget productions are tempted to use real guns on stage.
NEVER USE REAL GUNS ON STAGE!
Even if they are never loaded, there is always the danger that someone doing mischief will improperly load it with a blank or that there is a round in the chamber even though it appears to be unloaded. It is really really really unsafe to use real weaponry.

Many people solve that problem by using a track starter pistol, But a starter pistol has a very specific look, so it is often an improper prop for anything but an off stage sound effect. Also even guns that use blanks eject a good amount of debris and when used (even accidentally) at close range injuries do happen. Best bet, if a gun is am important prop for the show and it must be more than a visual - rent a proper stage gun from a Stage and film prop company. These guns are exact replicas and any type and period of gun can be rented and the safety advantage is immeasurable. These guns are rigged to load exactly like real guns but they are in the nature of cap guns and no debris will be ejected. Regardless, pointing any gun directly at anyone should be done with full control and awareness – not in play.

Swords –

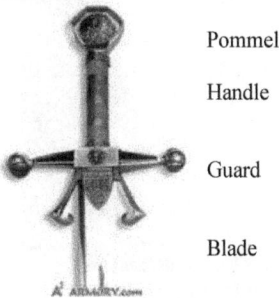

Pommel

Handle

Guard

Blade

Inside the handle is a piece of metal called the tang, which needs to be as strong as the blade itself. If not they snap at the handle easily in a sword fight and create shrapnel. So using those decorative swords meant to hang on the wall for anything more than carrying is not a good idea.

Most swords have removable handles and guards so you can use the same blade and slide on the type of guard that is best for the time period you are working in. (unscrew the pommel, slip off the handle and guard , slip on the new one and re-screw the pommel) Typical sword choices are:

Foil   **Sabre**

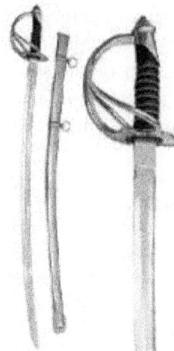

Rapier   **Broadsword**

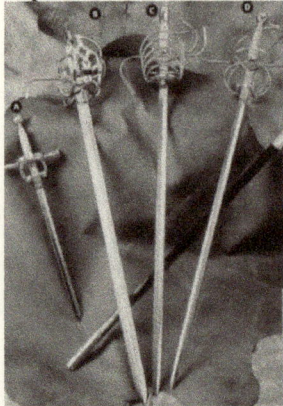 

 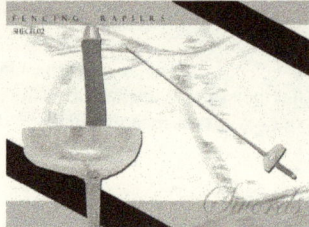

Samari   **Epee**

- Foils have a small blade that bends easily in a fight.
- Sabres are used when the choreography calls for "hacking
- Rapier is a flat blade and catches the light well its w perfect sword for musketeer stylized fighting.
- Broad swords MUST be all one piece of metal for safety
- Samari swords should all be made of one piece as well
- Epee are the ultimate choice for stage fighting and can do nearly anything choreographed.

Choreography –
In general choreography stems from the active fighter or the aggressor. Which in rehearsal results on the "victim energy" of the person attacked. For example in a sword fight the choreographer would block out an attack first and then a defense. This would be done slowly and with total control, until both parties had the choreography well memorized.

In unarmed combat the general procedure is to create spacing and distance so there is minimal or no contact at all. The aggressor controls the movement of punches or pulls through the use of isometrics, pantomime or stage illusion. While the defender snaps their head, bends in response, falls or grunts.

Some examples –
Slap across face: this is a very commonly used stage bit. If the actor being slapped isn't prepared and the aggressor actually slaps, a danger is (across jaw) broken teeth or (on the ear) broken ear drum. If an actual slap is used it should be on the neck (yes it will sting) and the victim snaps his head. If no actual contact is made sound can be achieved by having the defender raise his hand as if in response and the attacker actually hits the defenders hand as the defender snaps his head. Or replace the slap with the defender slapping his leg.

Punch: this requires repetition and practice for control. The attacker should pull the punch, at minimum an inch from the body of the defender who will need to show a strong physical reaction. A punch to the stomach needs to be pulled, the defender bends over. The attacker could then clasp his hands together and pull a hit to the back of the defender's neck (since the defender can't see and the hit it pulled he won't feel it a visual or loud noise needs to cue the defender's fall in response – foot stamp or grunt)

Repetition –
Stage combat moves should be worked in slow motion daily, the sequence of events should be talked through by all parties and then written down. Continue to repeat in slow motion until the natural familiarity with the moves indicates it is appropriate to speed up. Even after the sequence is comfortable, it should be run through before every performance. It is helpful if the combat partners learn to telegraph the blows as well – center of gravity, breathing and eye contact can insure both parties are aware and ready for the next movement.

PHOTO:Dack Viring and Zoe Carballa, Lou Labriola in "OTHELLO" **photographer Erin Thomas**

Hand Combat
More often than not you will be asked to work on some form of hand to hand combat. Here are some basic forms to practice before you find yourself in rehearsal and are asked to fall or hit someone without having a proper stage combat choreographer or a director who knows how to teach these moves.

THE FALL
You have been asked to trip or faint or react to a punch. You want to do the fall very SLOWLY the first time, sink (bend your knees and effect a "rubber" physical appearance) and get as close to the floor as you believably can, when you do drop aim at the thick and meaty parts of your body – thighs, shoulders, butt – and avoid the delicate breakable parts – like joints! If you must break your fall with your hands or knees avoid landing squarely on them and try to add in a way to slide or roll.

You can create a believable fall from the front, side or falling backward. But take the time to work through how to do it safely, run it on your own very slowly several times – using a mat if necessary then as you become more comfortable bring it up to speed. Now you can do the fall in rehearsal. The sooner you do this work on your own the better. Directors don't react well when they have blocked a scene and an actor stops to say "I haven't worked on that part yet". They may pressure you to just go ahead and do it – that is when injuries happen. So protect yourself and do your homework.

THE SLAP
As I mention before a real slap if placed wrong can break teeth, a jaw or an ear drum so don't just flail! Begin with talking the movement through with your scene partner (the one you will hit or who will hit you) define an area that gives you both a "margin of safety"- close enough to look like you COULD hit each other but actually only leave your fingertips millimeters away. Begin by not actually touching and mime the slap. 1. Make eye contact 2. Breath in to communicate that you are about to swing. 3. Throw the slap and 4. The victim reacts with energy.

If your director or scene partner want physical contact to happen the slap should happen on the thick part of the neck – it will sting and make the appropriate noise but it will avoid the potential places on the face that can be injured easily. The reaction of the person being hit is crucial to making this slap appear to be on the cheek – they need to have the attacker communicate the movement clearly – eye contact, breathing and swing. They also need to sharply turn or spin in the correct direction. This move should be practiced together before every rehearsal in preparation for the scene – not left to an "in the moment" movement.

THE PUNCH
Much of the same process goes into a punch. Begin by creating a margin of safety with your partner. Communicate the punch with eye contact, breath and swing. THERE IS NO SAFE PLACE to actually punch someone. The key to making this happen is timing of the attacker and reaction of the defender – that is only refined through practice practice practice! For adding in the sound of the punch (or slap) yells, grunts and moans cover

easily. The defender can clap his hands just as the hit is supposed to happen to create the sound, or the attacker could actually hit the defender's hand (open palm) to create sound as well.

It is very important to choreograph whatever you do, walk through the movement slowly and then build up to a realistic speed as both partners get comfortable. This is not a time to improvise EVER! Cueing the reaction of a "blind side" punch needs to be worked out between the partners as well. For example, if the attacker wants to hit the defender's stomach (causing him to bend forward) then hit the defender's back of neck dropping him to the floor – best way to communicate the back of the neck hit (since the defender is looking at the floor – not at his partner) is to cue the hit with a foot movement or something the defender can see so they know when to react.

OTHER CREATIVE PHYSICAL BITS

Tipping a chair while climbing – if you use a strong straight legged chair, you can literally balance the chair on it's back legs with one instep on the front edge of the seat and one instep on the edge of the top of the back of the chair. Step up on the chair (with feet positioned as just described) and slowly tip the chair back – with practice you can balance there and then ride the chair all the way to the floor

Dragging by the hair – the attacker grabs a handful of the defender's hair with his right, his left hand can grab the neckline of the costume (covered with hair it will appear both hands are holding hair. The defender grabs the attacker's wrist and holds themselves so that no actual hair pulling takes place.

Tripping – a believable way to trip (when nothing is there) is to catch the toe of one foot on the back of the ankle of the other foot for just an instant – enough time to throw off your stride naturally. When you try to catch yourself exaggerate the resulting lunge just a bit.

REMINDER-

WITH ALL PHYSICAL STAGE BITS YOU MUST PLAN, PRACTICE and communicate with your scene partner. Run through all physical bits as a part of your warm-up to rehearsal and before each performance to be most safe. Both attacker and defender must feel comfortable, safe and satisfied with the movement. It then needs to be written as choreography and rehearsed. There is no improvisation in stage combat.

Stage Combat Quiz
Please type this on a separate sheet of paper

1. **Real guns work fine for stage use.**

      True   False

2. Three elements of stage combat that need to be focused on are:

3. 1._____ 2._____
   3._____

4. **Name the parts of a sword**

    1._____   2._____

    3._____   4._____

5. **Name the two preferred stage weapons.**

    1._____   2._____

6. **Where is contact made is a stage slap?**

_____

7. **The most important aspect of any stage combat is:**

_____

8. **When performing unarmed stage combat use control and always _____ your blows.**

9. **What is the margin of safety?**

_____

_____

10. Armed stage combat is always choreographed from the _____point of view.

   11.   Describe one sequence of stage combat that we worked on in class. Describe fully. Use a separate piece of paper to write this.

CHAPTER EIGHT: Improvisational Theater

Improvisational Theatre (also known as **improv** or **impro**) is a form of theatre in which the actors perform spontaneously, without a script. Improvisation has been employed in live theatre at least since 16th century Commedia Dell'arte. Modern improvisation began in the classroom with the theatre games of Viola Spolin and Keith Johnstone in the 1950s, then evolved quickly to become an independent artform worthy of presentation before a paying audience. These forms can be seen locally at Geva Theater's Next Stage, television's "Whose Line Is It?" or comedy clubs and are often called "theater Sports" since the idea of competition is also added.

In all forms of improvisation, the actors invent/discover the dialogue and action as they perform. The unpredictable nature of such a performance lends itself naturally to comedy, and the majority of improvisational theatre is comedic, not dramatic. Dramatic improvisation is used by many companies and artists as a means of generating content for later performance. This is sometimes referred to as *"organic"* theatre, and is especially favored by creators of political theatre, experimental theatre, and practitioners of drama therapy. Improvisation is often used in actor training. Modern improvisational comedy, as it is practiced in the West, falls generally into two categories: short form and long form.

Improv process

Improvisational theatre allows an interactive relationship with the audience. Improv groups frequently solicit suggestions from the audience as a source of inspiration, a way of getting the audience involved, and as a means of proving that the performance is not scripted. That charge is sometimes aimed at the masters of the art, whose performances can seem so detailed that viewers may suspect the scenes were planned. In some ways it is. When a person skilled in improve takes that stage they already have developed a range of tried and true "bits" that they apply to the new situations. They have already developed a variety of characters, memorized punch lines and know a stock of traditional jokes before taking on the new ideas.

In order for an improvised **scene** to be successful, the actors involved must work together responsively to define the parameters and action of the scene. With each spoken word or action in the scene, an actor makes an *offer*, meaning that he or she defines some element of the reality of the scene. This might include giving another character a name, identifying a relationship, location, or using **mime** to define the physical environment. These activities are also known as *endowment*. It is the responsibility of the other actors to accept the offers that their fellow performers make; to not do so is known as **blocking**, in improve this means rejecting something offered it is not the kind of blocking a director uses for movement but psychological block) which usually prevents the scene from developing. Some performers may deliberately block (or otherwise break out of character) for comedic effect -- this is known as *gagging* -- but this generally prevents the scene from advancing and is frowned upon by many improvisers (traditional actors see this as breaking character and is considered a sign of poor theater skills – an embarrassment). Accepting an offer is usually accompanied by adding a new offer, often building on the earlier one; this is a process improvisers refer to as *"Yes, And..."* and is considered the cornerstone of improvisational technique. For example, an improv scene might begin with these lines.

Adam: I'm proud of all the work you've done here on the farm, Junior.

Bill: Yes, and I'm proud of you for giving up the moonshine, Pa.

PHOTO: Dr. Simon Carmel and Joseph Fox in "Windows"
photographer: Peter Haggerty

The unscripted nature of improv also implies no predetermined knowledge about the props that might be useful in a scene. Improv companies may have at their disposal some number of readily accessible props that can be called upon at a moment's notice, but many improvisers eschew props in favor of the infinite possibilities available through mime. As with all improv *offers*, actors are encouraged to respect the validity and continuity of the imaginary environment defined by themselves and their fellow performers; this means, for example, taking care not to walk through the table or "miraculously" survive multiple bullet wounds from another improviser's gun.

Because improv actors may be required to play a variety of roles without preparation, they need to be able to construct characters quickly with physicality, gestures, accents, voice changes, or other techniques as demanded by the situation. The actor may be called upon to play a character of a different age or sex. Character motivations are an important part of successful improv scenes, and improv actors must therefore attempt to act according to the objectives that they believe their character seeks. Just as a professional dancer is familiar with basic steps and common combinations of steps, a professional improve actor already has these elements and practices developing these elements – they do not truly depend on being spontaneously brilliant.

Many improvisational actors also work as scripted actors, and "improv" techniques are often taught in standard acting classes. The basic skills of listening, clarity, confidence, and performing without thinking are considered important skills for actors to develop.

How to build a scene –

Exposition –be sure to establish when, where, who and what is happening

Conflict – create a problem

Climax – allow the conflict to escalate into a physical extreme (chase, fight, etc.)

Resolution – tie up loose ends and find a way to close the scene

How to build a character –

Determine the outline of the character by defining (PIMP) physical shape, idiosyncrasies, motivation and psychology. As the scene goes on color in the details as you are able.

Game of Emotion –

Purpose: to discover ways to believably shift emotional responses quickly and smoothly.

How To Play: any conversation will do, perhaps one about shopping, during the conversation the audience suggests different emotions and without changing the topic of conversation the actors shift clearly into the emotion suggested.

Yes, No, Maybe –

Purpose: To develop a more instinctive approach to scene work and to disengage from dependence on text.

How To Play: #1 in your improve do not allow yourself to say those three words yes, no, maybe. #2 do a scene using only those words yes, no maybe

Zoo –

Purpose to unleash the instinctive actor and give access to the unconscious

How To Play: use a situation you know well and only communicate with animal sounds or gibberish

PHOTOS: Improvisation scene work from "Windows of the Soul" photographer: Julie Busch

Improvisation Crossword

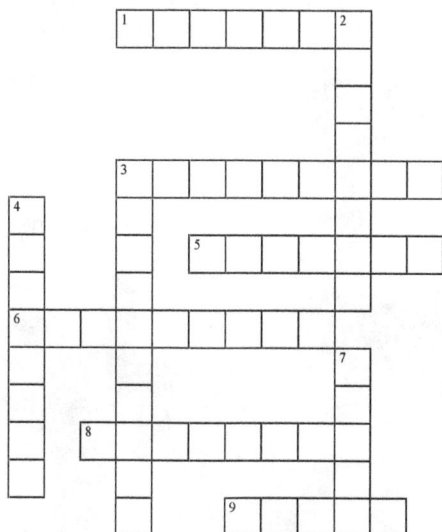

ACROSS

1 When political theater, experimental theater or drama therapy uses improvisation techniques

3 When an actor define the playing space by setting up furniture or other physical aspects

5 When an actor blocks information or breaks character

6 Where Viola Spolin and Keith johnson first used improv in 1950

8 When two or more people talk on stage

9 When an actor adds a fact to the scene

DOWN

2 The short way of saying commedia dell'Arte the 16th century performance style that began improv

3 The beginning of a play when you learn who, what, when and where

4 When an actor rejects new information or breaks character (different from movement on stage)

7 A short section of a full play determined by exits and entrances or location changes

Pick one of the photos below (from rehearsals of "Windows of the Soul" photographer Julie Busch) You need to decide what the characters are doing, what the problem is and how to resolve the problem. You will be expected to use someone in class to partner you. You will have only a few minutes to discuss how you want to perform.

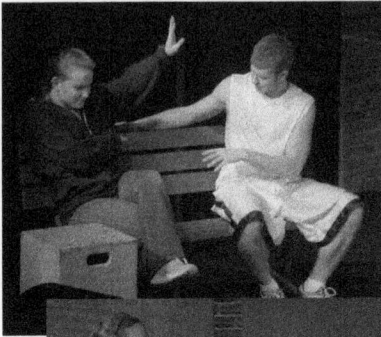

Who are these people?

Where are they?

What is the problem?

How does this story end?

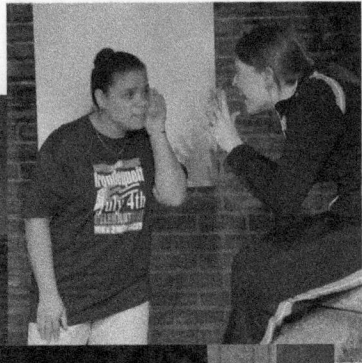

CHAPTER NINE: Alexander Technique

"The Alexander Technique is a method that works to change (movement) habits in our everyday activities. It is a simple and practical method for improving ease and freedom of movement, balance, support and coordination. The technique teaches the use of the appropriate amount of effort for a particular activity, giving you more energy for all your activities. It is not a series of treatments or exercises, but rather a reeducation of the mind and body. The Alexander Technique is a method which helps a person discover a new balance in the body by releasing unnecessary tension. It can be applied to sitting, lying down, standing, walking, lifting, and other daily activities..." - This quote is from Jane Alexander

Photo:googleimages

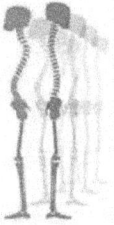

We all have unconscious movement habits. Without realizing it, we put undue pressure on ourselves. We use more force than we need to lift a coffee pot or a weight bar. We slouch as we sit, unaware that our way of doing things gives our bodies a certain look. We blame body problems on activities -- carpal tunnel syndrome on computer work, tennis elbow on tennis. But often it is how we do something that creates the problem, not the activity itself.

An Alexander Technique teacher helps you see what in your movement style contributes to your recurring difficulties -- whether it's a bad back, neck and shoulder pain, restricted breathing, perpetual exhaustion or limitations in performing a task or sport. Analyzing your whole movement pattern -- not just your symptom -- the teacher alerts you to habits of compression in your characteristic way of sitting, standing and walking. He or she then guides you -- with words and a gentle, encouraging touch -- to move in a freer, more integrated way.

The Technique's basic idea is that when the neck muscles do not overwork, the head balances lightly at the top of spine. The relationship between the head and the spine is of utmost importance. How we manage that relationship has ramifications throughout the rest of the body. As the boss -- good or bad -- sets the tone for an organization, the head / spine relationship -- compressed or free -- determines the quality of the body's overall coordination. Our neuromuscular system is designed to work in concert with gravity. Delicate poise of the head sparks the body's anti-gravity response: a natural oppositional force in the torso that easily guides us upward and invites the spine to lengthen, rather than compress, as we move. Instead of slouching or holding ourselves in a rigid posture, we can learn to mobilize this support system and use it wherever we go -- in the car, at the computer, in the gym.

Young children have this natural poise. If you watch a toddler in action, you will see an erect spine, free joints and a large head balancing easily on a little neck. A healthy child walks and

plays with regal posture. Barring birth defects, we all began that way. But over the years, we often lose that spontaneity and ease.

Using the Alexander Technique, you can learn to strip away harmful habits, heighten your self-awareness, and use your thought process to restore your original poise. In a way, you are learning something that, deep down, your body already knows. With the Alexander Technique, you come to understand much more about how your body works, and how to make it work for you. You can tap more of your internal resources, and begin on a path to enhancing your comfort and pleasure in all your activities.

Psychological Techniques like "the Method" lead to examining your inner life. You want to be able to access memories so you can apply those same emotions and understandings to your creation of a character. This invisible part of yourself is called:

Inner Life

	ME +	ME -
OTHERS −	2. Known to others, but not to me	3. Not known to me or to others
OTHERS +	1. Known to me and others	4. Known to me, but not to others

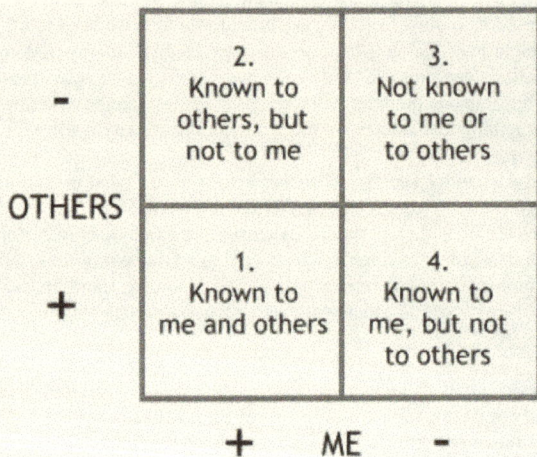

1. **The public area** contains things that are openly known and talked about - and which may be seen as strengths or weaknesses. This is the self that we choose to share with others
2. **The hidden area** contains things that others observe that we don't know about. Again, they could be positive or negative behaviours, and will affect the way that others act towards us.
3. **The unknown area** contains things that nobody knows about us - including ourselves. This may be because we've never exposed those areas of our personality, or because they're buried deep in the subconscious.

4. **The private area** contains aspects of our self that we know about and keep hidden from others.

Alexander Technique can give you a physical foundation for this understanding of "inner life" and provide you with habits that will allow you to use your body as the artistic instrument and actor or performer needs.

Misusing your body in any way prevents you from full developing your stage skills in: acting, puppetry, mask work, dance, gymnastics, juggling, Sign Language

Exercises:

Reach for a shoe thrown across the room –

Observe how each person reaches differently. The head is 12-15 pounds and rests on a tiny vertebrae. Compressing the spine leads to pain which will appear on stage as inhibition, nerves, fear, shyness and other emotions that cause stage fright and block access to deep emotion.

Now throw shoe again and lift it-

Head lifted, neck free, lengthen your body, legs support, arms float

1) Notice we all actually start to move before starting "rev up" change that moment to a place to breath and think
2) Place your feet fully on the floor – not up on your toes
3) Keep your knees over your toes
4) Tilt your head toward the object you are lifting
5) Bend at your hips

Wall Walk –

Walk you hands up and down the walls – think about the hand that is holding your balance not the hand that is moving

1) Remove tension from your wrist
2) Lengthen your neck
3) Hold your head lightly

4) Keep your shoulders even

Chair lift and sit –

Sit with a relaxed and lifted posture, observe how you transition to standing

1) Lift your neck and lengthen you back
2) Move to the edge of the seat
3) Place feel fully on the floor
4) Lean forward using your hips and lead with your head to stand

Homework #9

Blending Improvisation with Alexander technique for performance

Find a partner to work with pick one of the exercises described below and create a short scene. Be prepared to demonstrate these improvisational movement scenes in class.

- **Delsarte's Poses:** In a more advanced group we borrow from Delsarte's poses in order to create an exercise. (Shawn, 1954:45) The first person mimes a situation, freezing at any given point. This is similar to the child's game of statues: it is also mentioned in Genevieve Stebbins work in American Delsartism (Stebbins 1885). The next person copies the freeze and moves that pose into another activity. For example: a person mimes bowling and freezes at the moment of letting go of the ball (with right arm extended, palm facing up, knees bent.) The next person assumes that pose and mimes asking for a handout. This is also a process used for American Sign Language story telling and poetic techniques (Gannon 1981:357)

- **Role Playing:** Each member of the group borrows another actor's physical expression or movement and then shifts back to herself. In an intermediate level, one actor copies someone else's movements in the production they are currently working on. They are limited to only two or three movements to make it clear whom they are illustrating. At more advanced levels, they illustrate only those characters that are American Delsarte examples of character types. The three basic types I mentioned in the introduction are used In brief: intellectual types have their center of gravity high, their sign or gesture choices are detailed, specific and often expressed high – near the face, their movements are sharp and staccato. Emotional types have their center of gravity in the chest area, their sign or gesture choices are fluid, smooth and often expressed at chest level. Physical types have their center of gravity low and into the hips. Their sign or gesture choices are fists or open hands and are often expressed in the lower abdomen area. The technique of role shifting is common in American Sign Language and is discussed at some length in the Registry of Interpreters for the Deaf (RID) Newsletter *VIEWS* (June 2001). By using Delsarte's full body charts as shown in *Every Little Movement* (Shawn, 1954) to help define and improve physical choices this exercise becomes quite a challenge.

- **Mirror Game:** Partners pair up to do a basic mirror game, but the leadership is shared. One partner begins leading but communicates with the following partner only through movement and eye contact. When the follower wishes to take over that is communicated using only energy or eye movement to indicate the shift – no speaking. In intermediate levels, the partners close their eyes and try to feel the movement through energy; some touch is acceptable to help the partners connect with each other. This might also have to be preceded by allowing one person to stand with her eyes closed and allow their partner to pass his hands over her body. The person who has their eyes closed can often be aware of where her partner is focusing even without sound, sight, or touch. Many people find this intimate and rather difficult even though no actual touch is happening. At advanced levels, the partners stand back to back and move in similar ways. Videotaping can show the actors exactly how closely alike they move. Often they already know when they were connected and when not, but watching the video tape offers visible confirmation.

Centering – centering (Zen meditation, akido, circus juggler) absorb energy include the energy into your new center – do the bonding with the drum.

Slow-motion tag play without rules, then walk them through imagining walking through custard, play again. Easier – because of the mind-imagination. Acting needs you to surround yourself with imagery.
Paradox – serious fun – it is legal to have fun!

CHAPTER TEN: Del-Sign

A theatrical fusion of cultures using François Delsarte codified movement and American Sign Language

Del-Sign is an experimental technique that combines the foundations of Delsarte's concepts with the structure of American Sign Language to create an external (physical) approach to acting. It is not intended to replace the techniques an individual actor already has in place; it is intended as a way to round-out or complete the presentational vocabulary of the actor or speaker so that they can approach the work in a more informed way. (Photo above is "Windows of the Soul" cast at NTID 1510 Theater Lab, photographer: Amber Stuhler)

So is this Experimental Theater?

When people say "experimental theater" they often seem to think the word experimental means *new* or *nonrealistic* or *weird*. But in fact, what makes it experimental is exactly the same thing that makes experimental physics experimental – that it proceeds by means of *experiments*, by people trying things out to see what works, rather than by holding to a belief in a system, or by dedicating themselves to one or another theory or aesthetic. To that end yes, it is experimental.

(photo: Nakita Smith and Gabrielle Nocciolino in "Sign-Arella" photographer: Erin Thomas)

Del-Sign combines Francois Delsarte codified movement techniques and American Sign Language.

Who is Delsarte?

Francois Delsarte (photo: googleimages.com)

Was born in 1811 and was an orphan by the age of nine. He made his way in the world by rag picking. Pere Bambini took the poor little boy under his wing and discovered Francois' natural musical talents. Bambini enrolled the boy in the Conservatory for Music in Paris. Delsarte had a hard time at the Conservatory as he felt that his instructors were unable to teach him a truthful way to present his art. At that time students were expected to imitate the master without analyzing the technical components of their style.

Regardless of this problem in training, Delsarte became a regular principle performer with the Lyric Opera in Paris. It was there that tragedy struck. Due to poor vocal training Delsarte lost his voice. Fearful of losing his job (and financial security) he continued to perform. Opera was not the sedate performance style we know today. In Delsarte's day it was noisy and busy with the audience watching itself as much as they watched the stage. Delsarte's physical interpretation of his roles was so compelling that no one noticed he wasn't singing for quite some time.

Although his abilities created a sensation, Delsarte chose to continue to study what he called, The Natural Laws of Expression. He spent time watching people in all types of situations, children at play, wives waiting for word of their husbands after a mine collapse, deathbed watches, etc. All this to see how people naturally expressed themselves. It is speculated that he even spent time in the French Deaf Community in Paris at that time. He went even further by studying physiology and taking part in autopsies. He found that there is a common physical form of communication regardless of language or cultural background.

He broke his findings into the Law of Trinity

"The unity of three things, each of which is essential to the other two, each co-existing in time, co-penetrating in space, a co-operative in motion. Many religions have the concept of the Trinity, most notably the Hindu with its Brahma, Siva and Vishnu. So it is with representing life. In the case of the performance it is essential TO KNOW, TO DO AND TO BE."

Delsarte as quoted in Ted Shawn's EVERY LITTLE MOVEMENT (graphic on right appears in "Every Little Movement" graphic available through Lincoln Center Performing Arts Library)

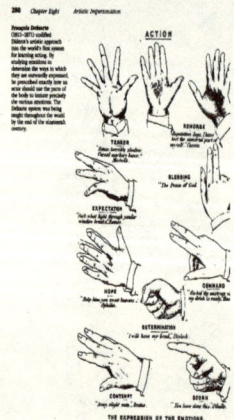

As with anything popular, Delsarte's technique was turned to kitch soon after his death in 1871. He was virtually a National hero to the French. Several of his students came to America and began to teach the technique here. Steele Macaye and Mrs. Hovey were the only true teachers of the original concept. Most of my knowledge of Delsarte's technique comes from their writings on the subject. Delsarte himself, never wrote anything down for as we know from a personal letter written to his daughter in 1868:

"I do believe that my concept of the Laws of Nature are ever developing. I am therefore loath to write them down thereby freezing the concept in time and in turn creating an untruth."

By 1880 Delsarte's interest in the truth was drowned in a flood of pseudo-Delsarte teachers who took the basic tenants, the basic exercises and turned them into a "gymnastic". As the technique became more and more distilled it faced more and more derision. Not surprisingly for our purposes Delsarte's technique was given a fresh breath of life when Albert Ballin (a notable Deaf author) used his knowledge of Delsarte's technique to teach two Deaf girls performing in the Silent movies of the time a performance piece. The performance was heralded as "truthful", "wondrous", but the fact that the performers were Deaf somehow discredited their use of Delsarte's technique and it was considered a fluke (this story is related in THE DEAF MUTE HOWLS by Albert Ballin)

AMERICAN SIGN LANGUAGE IN THEATER

ASL and Deaf performers have a long and detailed history of performance and storytelling. Many of the greatest contributions have been made by theatre companies which focus on Deaf performers and audiences namely; The National Theater for the Deaf, among many others. I would encourage you to go see the work of other companies which use American Sign Language in performance: The New York Deaf Theater and Deaf West to name a few.

For our purposes ASL has many applications. ASL grammar: the proper facial expression is tantamount to proper punctuation. Eye contact and focus is not only used for human contact and communication but also as a way of establishing character and reference points. ASL structure: requires the signer to have a very visual frame of reference. Rather than focusing on beauty of sounds ASL focuses on beauty of images. There are specific constructions which use a term "cinematic" meaning the idea of describing with long shots and close shots similar to how a movie will tell a visual story. As one of my mentors George Garcia often points out the world is becoming more visually based soon the division between "hearing" and Deaf will melt in a common goal toward a visual world. Take for example the technique often used in Story Sign of role shifting. That is, when a person tells a story s/he take on the characters rather than going with the construct of "he said" "she said". This is a common tool used on stage by actors which have no knowledge of ASL. As obvious as it may seem ASL is crucial to the development of stage performance in that the "voice" of the language or emotive tone, is facial expression, body language and gesture. ASL combines these elements in a highly refined way to physically produce communication of higher concepts. These are the same tools that actors need to refine in order to make the emotional subtext of the character shine through.

Although Delsarte did not know Sign, his point of view is in direct synch:

"Gesture is the direct agent of the heart, the persuasive agent. The language of the hand is a universal language; some communication can be made with descriptive pantomime, but many gestures are universal "words". We all recognize the hand movements which say "come here", "hello", "good-bye". I am sure the list is virtually limitless. Gesture has been given to man to reveal what speech is powerless to express. If we desire that a thing shall always be remembered, we must not say it in speech; we must let it be divined in gesture. Gestures relate us to other beings, expressing our emotions, from the highest to the lowest."
     THE ACTOR'S ART,ed. Sir John Alexander
Hammerton (photo on right is from Deaf West's Broadway production of "Big River" reprint permission: Deaf West Inc.)

Pictured above - is a scene from the Deaf West Broadway production of "Big River" this revival of a musical was deemed an entirely new approach and staging concepts often used in Del-Sign were employed by the director, most particularly with the role of Papp. This could be the result of a "common consciousness" within the creative world but given that a director's vision is often brought to life in combination with the artistic staff and colored by the actor's interpretation - some of the "coloring" was no doubt contributed by six of the original cast members who had worked in the Del-Sign style previous to work with Deaf West. Although three of the actors were in the chorus and would not have had any influence, the other three; Guthrie Nutter (Twelfth Night) Michelle Banks (Noises Off) Iosif Schniederman (Noises Off, Tempest) all had principle roles and Iosif was originally cast as Papp. He was injured in the opening performance by a set piece and replaced early in the run of the show. However, he has since described how his suggestion in rehearsal to consider doubling the role in Del-Sign style was accepted. (see also New York Times Sunday August 3, 2003 Art Section, letter to the Editor "Blending Cultures")

I'm of two minds! And so are you.

Until recently corporate America wasn't doing much to take advantage of one of them. But now that we are hip-deep in what has been called both the "Creative Economy" and the "Conceptual Age," no one can afford to ignore the artist within; the right hemisphere of the brain.

Each side of the brain plays its own role in cognition. But the artistic or right brain-imaginative side of the thought process has traditionally been marginalized in corporate America as well as in the rest of our culture. (photo on left is from Deaf Jam Poetry, photographer: Luane Davis Haggerty)

Even here at RIT! On a campus that celebrates innovation the creative arts are limited. Although limited resources can inspire creativity I look forward to a time when creativity can explore the full possibilities of its power. Witness the power of the NTID Drama program. Although we do not have a department (we are a program) nor do we offer a major, NTID Performing Arts is the featured presenter at most "visual theater" conferences across the nation, our students have appeared on major television, commercial and film venues; and our approach to communication issues, conflict resolution and leadership has been widely published and emulated. "When you don't have money you need to have ideas!" (Quincey Jones). Imagine what more we can do when Right and left brain, technical and artistic are more equally balanced. We truly will balance "to make a living and live a life".

Del-Sign bridges cultural gaps allowing Deaf and hearing actors to work very closely together. It is a model for other cross-cultural collaborations. As the global economy gathers strength, the need to work with others who may not share the same language, cultural habits or behaviors and have widely different perspectives on life increases. American higher education does a wonderful job of educating the left side of the brain, which contains the human language center and is the outspoken, logical, linear half of the cognitive equation. But more training needs to be given to the right brain, home of spatial perception and nonverbal concepts. This right brain thinking is the nonlinear, high-concept source of imagination and pleasure. (photo above Anthony Bruccato performs in "Read our Lips" photographer: Luane Davis Haggerty)

Del-Sign physically balances both cultures and languages which, when represented at the same time, create the metaphor of parallel worlds. Once the physical muscle memory is engaged, the cognitive memory and integration of new ideas flows more easily

Del-Sign engages many of our high-concept, high touch muscles improving communication and brain-storming. The imaginative abilities that Del-Sign improves have always been a part of what it means to be human. It's just that after a few generations in the Information Age, many of our high concept, high-touch muscles have atrophied. The change is to work them back into shape.

Why make use of this technique?

Now that we've entered the era of the "creative economy" and the "Conceptual Age" no one can afford to ignore the artist within. For our students entering the workforce at this place and time it is crucial to have a base and a technique for applying the technical skills they have acquired to innovative approaches. The face of American Industry is changing.

Left-brain-centric work, meaning computer programming, financial accounting, routing calls - is now done more cheaply in Asia or more efficiently by computers. If it can be outsourced or automated, it probably has been. Creativity can't be outsourced or outdated. Equipment needs replacement – creativity just needs a safe place to play!

Left and right brain both need to be engaged for new ideas to form – balanced learning, analysis and communication are just some of the results.

"All business is in the Art business"
Robert A. Lutz, Chair of product development for General Motors

Robert A. Lutz is the CEO in charge of product development at General Motors. As he stated in an article for the New York Times "I see us as being in the art business, arts, entertainment and mobile sculpture, which coincidentally, also provides transportation." When a car company like GM is in the art business, every company in any other industry is also. (New York Times 4/13, Business Section)

What did we just do and why?

Some of the activities or exercises that this chapter will introduce you to were developed in order to create an Energy Framework for the work of skill building in Del-Sign. Although the physical aspects of these activities are accessible to anyone the conceptual element are more complex and require more serious study. Practice in these techniques while understanding their connection to an Energy Framework derived from quantum theory, ancient Chinese philosophies on energy and physical movement/communication activities used in American Sign Language and in the codified movement work of Delsarte will result in opening the student to a vocabulary that open the mind to the ideas living outside of the box. Fu-His, who sets the pattern for reflection, as described in the earliest Chinese legends from around 3000 BC, invents the eight trigrams devised from the yin and yang duality observed in the cosmos. His initial efforts to comprehend the virtue of all beings in all creations have led to the *Book of Changes* (*I-Ching*), *Taoist's Book* (*Tao-Te-Ching*) by Lao-Tsu, the work of Chuang-Tsu, *The Four Books* by Confucius (Kong-Fu-Tsu) and Mencius, and *The Art of War* by Sun-Tsu. When study in this technique deepens, these activities help to illustrate the nature of reality as a discrete energy of opposites. It uses energies symbolized by "trigrams" to unfold meanings which can allow us to make use of both right and left brain concepts. This fusion of techniques and theories explains the nature of innovation as energy, that flows in complement with each other to achieve success.

Delsarte focused on an overall approach to his work – To Know, To Do and To be

Information on the *I'Ching* thanks to Carolyn Yu of the Antioch University Ph.D. Program

TO KNOW -

- The Chinese accredit the origin of the *I-Ching* (or *Yi-jing* or *Book of Changes*, or 易經), to Fu Hsi (or Fu Xi), who lived about 3000 BCE. He purportedly recognized that the fundamental energies are derivatives of yin (negative) and yang (positive) polarity. This legendary sage's work asserts all events and relationships in the cosmos are expressible in terms of nature's energies. When events and relationships manifest, they express themselves as two inseparable, complementary, coexisting energies. This philosophy begins with *Tai ji* (or *Tai-Chi* or 太極). Secter equates *Tai-Chi* with the "Supreme Ultimate, that Unmanifest Essence which is the universe itself" (Secter, 1993, p, 18).

- The concept of Yin and Yang: Yang (陽), discloses itself as "active, firm, light, initiative, contractive, immaterial, affirming, turned on, sustaining, and positive" while Yin (陰), as "passive, dark, material, yielding, soft expansive, nourishing, pliable, turned off, and negative" (Secter, 1993, p, 18). A dualistic universe, however, consists of varying degrees of difference. As yang energy is likened to days and yin energy to nights in the nature's order. Within each, there is an element of the other—in bright daylight, there is shadow or darkness, within the night shines the brightness of the moon and stars.

This parallels the Del-Sign concept of partner work on stage. Exercises to enhance this duality in a concrete reality include:

- Eye contact and breathing: the entire group inhales and exhales together in an exaggerated manner three times. Then one person who makes eye contact and exhales starts the breath, the person with whom they made eye contact inhales changes focus and exhales. This continues around the circle. As the cast becomes more familiar with the activity and the show, the breath can suggest a gesture or a mimed object that is related to the show in some way. For example: blowing bubbles, exhaling a cigarette, sneezing, blowing a kiss, or throwing a basketball. As the actors become more advanced, the breath incorporates lines from the show. This activity can be used with scene partners, as well, outside of a general warm-up. It is of interest to reiterate how this activity combines aspects of both Delsarte Systems and American Sign Language. The rhythmic breath and control are similar to those mentioned by Shawn (1954) while the structure of the exercise-standing in a circle and emphasis on eye contact is appropriate to deaf cultural habits (Gannon, 1989).

TO DO -

- *Trigram energy: Heaven—Founding, Paternal*

- This represents energy moving straight, upward or forward, as an advancing force that may, and can, ultimately push aside obstacles. This energy's qualities encompass resolution, judgment, power and will—tempered by experience, purity of intention, stature, and endurance. It is tireless, dispassionate, unemotional, and impassive with no time to waste. It is the field of universal energy and a spiritual, ethical mind force.

- *Trigram energy: Earth—Nurturing, Maternal*

- The energy movement of this trigram is that of mass and is the manifestation of essence. It is both receiving (accumulating) and sinking down into (absorbing). This energy is the polar opposite of Heaven energy; it sustains original creation and fosters new creativity expressing the need for the perfection of fulfillment and the endowment of substantive and material form. It is a cohesive collection of individual particulars—an assembled multiplicity.

- *Trigram energy: Wind—Influential, Cognizant*

- This energy moves curvaceously, sometimes quickly, sometimes slowly, with the ability to proceed in many directions at the same time. It is the polar opposite of Thunder. Constantly advancing and retreating, it is the most cerebral, unpredictable, and changeable energy. It has the capacity to simultaneously envelop and penetrate—often in ways that are comfortable and caressing. It is intense, proud, self-assured, resilient, and inviting, yet sensual, active and mature, permeating and yielding at the same time.

- *Trigram energy: River—Competitive, Contentious*

- This energy's movement is always falling, tumbling, flowing, streaming, or swirling down and around unpredictably. It represents the many atmospheric forms of water—rain, snow, sleet, hail—as well as water flowing on, and under, the ground toward a destination. It also connotes the effects of water erosion—canyons, abysses, caverns, and dry riverbeds. It is usually meandering yet still contained or confined in the same way that rivers are retained within their banks but continue to create a new path.

This parallels the Del-Sign activity of:

• Center of gravity characters: Although there are an infinite number of character types to be portrayed the essential element of them can be built upon where the character holds his center of gravity. Delsarte began with three character types: Intellectual- center of gravity high, detailed gesture and sharp movement. Emotional- center of gravity in the chest (expanded or concave) gestures are fluid and smooth, movement is graceful.. Physical – the center of gravity is in the hips gestures are punches or slices in the air, movement is animalistic and sensual.

• Role Playing: Each member of the group borrows another actor's physical expression or movement and then shifts back to herself. In an intermediate level, one actor copies someone else's movements in the production they are currently working on. They are limited to only two or three movements to make it clear whom they are illustrating. At more advanced levels, they illustrate only those characters that are American Delsarte examples of character types. The three basic types outlined by Delsarte are, in brief: intellectual types have their center of gravity high, their sign or gesture choices are detailed, specific and often expressed high – near the face, their movements are sharp and staccato. Emotional types have their center of gravity in the chest area, their sign or gesture choices are fluid, smooth and often expressed at chest level. Physical types have their center of gravity low and into the hips. Their sign or gesture choices are fists or open hands and are often expressed in the lower abdomen area. The technique of role shifting is common in American Sign Language and is discussed at some length in the Registry of Interpreters for the Deaf (RID) Newsletter *VIEWS* (June 2001). By using Delsarte's full body charts as shown in *Every Little Movement* (Shawn, 1954) to help define and improve physical choices the emotion and relationship of movement to the personality is explored without judgment allowing practice of cross-cultural understanding and communication.

TO BE

• Ancient Chinese *I-Ching* (*Book of Changes*), yin and yang philosophy and modern quantum theory share a common perspective—energy Quantum theory describes atomic movements in terms of transcendent matter in an energy field. The *I-Ching* explains events and actions as the consequence of energy polarity with variations caused by energy synchronicity resulting from opposition and complementarity. The *I-Ching* offers a rich point of reference; it links real life experiences with primal nature's energy. Del-Sign links real life experiences with analysis of character and nature.

APPENDIX of additional monologue choices

Review the monologues – chose one and prepare to recite the monologue in class
(Photo: Randal Jackson in "Othello" NTID Production. Photographer: Erin Thomas)

I have prepared these monologues for you. Most have images that can suggest the sort of person who is speaking and what the character might look like. I have provided an ASL Gloss for most of these and left room for you to write your own gloss on others. Do not feel you MUST follow the gloss it is intended simply as a way to get started on creating this monologue.

Many of these monologues are considered "standard" audition choices. Because the auditors will know these monologues it will be easier for them to watch you do them in ASL and still know what character you are portraying. This will give even hearing directors a sense that they can accurately judge your acting work even if they don't know ASL.

MEN'S MONOLOGUES

Emperor Jones by Eugene O'Neill
(photo: Troy Chapman and Christopher Coles in IRT production of Emperor Jones, photographer: Peter Haggerty)

Note: you are talking to Smithers a white man who is your assistant. When it is time for his lines image someone is saying that line and react. Then continue with you monologue.

JONES—(*with a contemptuous sniff*) I ain't no chicken-liver like you is. Trees an' me, we' se friends, and dar's a full moon comin' bring me light. And let dem po' niggers make all de fool spells dey'se a min' to. Does yo' s'pect I'se silly, enuff to b'lieve in ghosts an' ha'nts an' all dat ole woman's talk? G'long, white man! You ain't talkin' to me. (*with a chuckle*) Doesn't you know dey's got to do wid a man was member in good standin' o' de Baptist Church? Sho' I was dat when I was porter on de Pullmans, befo' I gits into my little trouble. Let dem try deir heathen tricks. De Baptist Church done pertect me and land dem all in hell. (*then with more confident satisfaction*) And I'se got little silver bullet o' my own, don't forgits.

SMITHERS—Ho! You 'aven't give much 'eed to your Baptist Church since you been down 'ere. I've 'card myself you 'ad turned yer coat an' was takin' up with their blarsted witch-docters, or whatever the 'ell yer calls the swine.

JONES—(*vehemently*) I pretends to! Sho' I pretends! Dat's part o' my game from de fust. If I finds out dem niggers believes dat black is white, den I yells it out louder 'n deir loudest. It don't git me nothin' to do missionary work for de Baptist Church. I'se after de coin, an' I lays my Jesus on de shelf for de time hem'. (*stops abruptly to look at his watch—alertly*) But I ain't got de time to waste no more fool talk wid you. I'se gwine away from heah dis secon'. (*He reaches in under the throne and pulls out an expensive Panama hat with a bright multi-colored band and sets it jauntily on his head.*) So long, white man! (*with a grin*) See you in jail sometime, maybe!

ENGLISH	ASL GLOSS
—(*with a contemptuous sniff*) I ain't no chicken-liver like you is. Trees an' me, we' se friends, and dar's a full moon comin' bring me light. And let dem po' niggers make all de fool spells dey'se a min' to. Does yo' s'pect I'se silly, enuff to b'lieve in ghosts an' ha'nts an' all dat ole woman's talk? G'long, white man! You ain't talkin' to me. (*with a chuckle*) Doesn't you know dey's got to do wid a man was member in good standin' o' de Baptist Church? Sho' I was dat when I was porter on de Pullmans, befo' I gits into my little trouble. Let dem try deir heathen tricks. De Baptist Church done pertect me and land dem all in hell. (*then with more confident satisfaction*) And I'se got little silver bullet o' my own, don't forgits.	You chicken – scared me/you same/ NOT! You white me black same night same trees, full moon appear shine light. Let them unimportant niggers creative magic spells all day/all night don't care. You think I foolish – I believe spirits real same as unimportant old women. Finifh white man. Talk with me finish. (laugh) I not believe spirit I good Baptist church person. I join Baptist when I work on trains as PORTER past before I stuck in jail. Allow them try magic tricks. Baptist Church will protect me from native religion. All unimportant native people will go to hell (confident) More protection have – I have silver bullet (show it) don't forget
(SMITHERS SAYS THIS) Ho! You 'aven't give much 'eed to your Baptist Church since you been down 'ere. I've 'card myself you 'ad turned yer coat an' was takin' up with their blarsted witch-docters, or whatever the 'ell yer calls the swine.	**Act like you are listening to this and react**
(*vehemently*) I pretends to! Sho' I pretends! Dat's part o' my game from de fust. If I finds out dem niggers believes dat black is white, den I yells it out louder 'n deir loudest. It don't git me nothin' to do missionary work for de Baptist Church. I'se after de coin, an' I lays my Jesus on de shelf for de time hem'. (*stops abruptly to look at his watch—alertly*) But I ain't got de time to waste no more fool talk wid you. I'se gwine away from heah dis secon'. (*He reaches in under the throne and pulls out an expensive Panama hat with a bright multi-colored band and sets it jauntily on his head.*) So long, white man! (*with a grin*) See you in jail sometime, maybe!	I fake believe spirits true I trick them. I play game trick unimportant native people. If they tell me they believe black equal white fine I accept and copy – fake – I yell louder to cover. I teach Baptist Christian religion – NOT! I benefit nothing. I want money. My goal money if Jesus show up I grab put Jesus on shelf continue goal money. (Looks at watch) Time run out finish silly talk talk finish, I pow out of here now! (grabs hat) bye white man! I see you future happen you/me both stuck jail (laugh) bye!

Seinfeld
"The ex-girlfriend"

By Larry David and Jerry Seinfeld

She can't kill me right? People break up all the time. It just didn't work out. What can I do? I wanted to love her. I tried to love her. I couldn't. I kept looking at her face. I'd go, "c'mon, love her. Love her."
I finally told her I loved her. I had no choice. She squeezed it out of me! She'd tell me she loved me. Alright, at first, I just look at her. I'd go "oh, really?" or "Boy, that's that's, something." But, eventually you have to come back with "Well, I love you." You know, you can only hold out for so long.
And I didn't even ask her out. She asked me out first. She called me up. What was I supposed to do, say no? I can't do that to someone. I'm a nice guy. (THEN SUDDENLY) And she seduced me! We were in my apartment. I'm sitting on the couch. She's on a chair. I get up to go to the bathroom. I come back. She's on the couch. What am I supposed to do, not do anything? I couldn't do that. I would've insulted her.
I had nothing to do with any of this! I met all her friends. I didn't want to meet them. I kept trying to avoid it. I knew it would only get me in deeper. But they were everywhere. They kept popping up, all over theplace. "This is Nancy, this is Susan, this is Amy. This is my cousin. This is my brother. This is my father." It's like I'm in quicksand.
Please! Do I have to break up with her in person? Can't I do it over the phone?

ENGLISH	ASL "Gloss"
She can't kill me right? People break up all the time. It just didn't work out. What can I do? I wanted to love her. I tried to love her. I couldn't. I kept looking at her face. I'd go, "c'mon, love her. Love her."	Girlfriend kill me can't. Right? People break-up break-up break-up. Relationship not success. Do-do? I want love girlfriend. I try love girlfriend. Can't I look her face continue.
I finally told her I loved her. I had no choice. She squeezed it out of me! She'd tell me she loved me. Alright, at first, I just look at her. I'd go "oh, really?" or "Boy, that's that's, something." But, eventually you have to come back with "Well, I love you." You know, you can only hold out for so long.	I think myself go ahead love her love ver "pah" I tell her I love you. Choice none. She force me. She tell me I love you First time I respond "really?" next time I respond " wow! Next next next "pah" I respond I love you. Can only fist-in-front-of-mouth short time.
And I didn't even ask her out. She asked me out first. She called me up. What was I supposed to do, say no? I can't do that to someone. I'm a nice guy. (THEN SUDDENLY) And she seduced me! We were in my apartment. I'm sitting on the couch. She's on a chair. I get up to go to the bathroom. I come back. She's on the couch. What am I supposed to do, not do anything? I	Past start how? She ask me date. She page me. I respond how? Must say no? Can't say no. I nice me.
Next happen what? She sleep with me Happen my apt. I sit couch. She sit chair. I go bathroom come back. She sit couch. Do-do? Freeze? Can't freeze. Insult her will.

couldn't do that. I would've insulted her. I had nothing to do with any of this! I met all her friends. I didn't want to meet them. I kept trying to avoid it. I knew it would only get me in deeper. But they were everywhere. They kept popping up, all over the place. "This is Nancy, this is Susan, this is Amy. This is my cousin. This is my brother. This is my father." It's like I'm in quicksand. Please! Do I have to break up with her in person? Can't I do it over the phone?	Blame me not me not responsible. Her friends meet meet meet. Don't want meet. Try try avoid. I know I meet friends relationship stuck. Her friends everywhere. Appear appear appear. Meet nancy, meet susan, meet Amy … meet cousin, meet brother meet FATHER!" I drown! Please! Don't want meet tell her break up. Don't mind I tell her break-up on VP?

RENT
Character name: MARK

We begin on Christmas Eve with me,
Mark, and my roommate, Roger.
We live in an industrial loft on the corner of 11th street and
Avenue B, the top floor of what was once a music publishing factory.
Old rock 'n' roll posters hang on the walls.
They have Roger's picture advertising gigs
at CBGB's and the Pyramid Club. We have an
illegal wood burning stove; its exhaust pipe crawls
up to a skylight.
All of our electrical appliances are plugged into one thick extension
cord which snakes its way out a window. Outside, a small tent city
has sprung up in the lot next to our building.
Inside, we are freezing because we have no heat.

[He turns the camera to ROGER]   Smile!

ENGLISH	ASL "Gloss"
We begin on Christmas Eve with me, Mark, and my roommate, Roger.	Happen story begin past Christmas EVE Me, Roger, my roommate
We live in an industrial loft on the corner of 11th street and	We live apt old building loft big apt Where? 11 Street cross Ave B
Avenue B, the top floor of what was once a music publishing factory.	Past old building publish music now two-of-us live top floor
Old rock 'n' roll posters hang on the walls.	Our apt decorated, posters have pictures old
They have Roger's picture advertising gigs at CBGB's and the Pyramid Club. We have an	rock and roll, one poster have my roommate picture ad for for club CBGB also Club
illegal wood burning stove; its exhaust pipe crawls	Pyramid. No heat we do do wood burn stove pipe for
up to a skylight.	smoke up and out window in roof
All of our electrical appliances are plugged	Electric things all plug one added chord

into one thick extension cord which snakes its way out a window. Outside, a small tent city has sprung up in the lot next to our building. Inside, we are freezing because we have no heat. [He turns the camera to ROGER] Smile!	That chord idea same snake out window Outside you see tent tent ten idea same small city Before empty area now pop up tents Inside we freeze, cold, why? No heat Smile roommate!

MERCHANT OF VENICE

LAUNCELOT: Certainly my conscience will serve me to run from this Jew my master. The fiend is at mine elbow and tempts me, saying to me, 'Gobbo, Launcelot Gobbo, good Launcelot,' or 'good Gobbo,' or 'good Launcelot Gobbo -- use your legs, take the start, run away.' My conscience says, 'No. Take heed, honest Launcelot; take heed, honest Gobbo,' or as aforesaid, 'honest Launcelot Gobbo -- do not run; scorn running with thy heels.' Well, the most courageous fiend bids me pack. 'Fia!' says the fiend; 'away!' says the fiend. 'For the heavens, rouse up a brave mind,' says the fiend, 'and run.' Well, my conscience hanging about the neck of my heart says very wisely to me, 'My honest friend Launcelot, being an honest man's son' -- or rather 'an honest woman's son,' for indeed my father did something smack, something grow to; he had a kind of taste -- Well, my conscience says, 'Launcelot, budge not.' 'Budge,' says the fiend. 'Budge not,' says my conscience. 'Conscience,' say I, 'you counsel well.' 'Fiend,' say I, 'you counsel well.' To be ruled by my conscience, I should stay with the Jew my master who, God bless the mark, is a kind of devil; and to run away from the Jew, I should be ruled by the fiend who, saving your reverence, is the devil himself. Certainly the Jew is the very devil incarnation; And in my conscience, my conscience is but a kind of hard conscience to offer to counsel me to stay with the Jew. The fiend gives the more friendly counsel. I will run, fiend; my heels are at your commandment; I will run.

ENGLISH	ASL "Gloss"
Certainly my conscience will serve me to run from this Jew my master. The fiend is at mine elbow and tempts me, saying to me, 'Gobbo, Launcelot Gobbo, good Launcelot,' or 'good Gobbo,' or 'good Launcelot Gobbo -- use your legs, take the start, run away.' My conscience says, 'No. Take heed, honest Launcelot; take heed, honest Gobbo,' or as aforesaid, 'honest Launcelot Gobbo -- do not run; scorn running with thy heels.' Well, the most courageous fiend bids me pack. 'Fia!' says the fiend; 'away!' says the fiend. 'For the heavens, rouse up a brave mind,' says the fiend, 'and run.' Well, my conscience hanging about the neck of my heart says very wisely to me, 'My honest	True biz my mind warns me my boss (jewish himself!) idea same evil my boss pulls my elbow Tells me (show many different ways of convincing you sweet, anger, best friend, father, begging) Good Gobbo Run ! escape but my mind tells me No! pay attention, I honest me, I good person, hard worker me. Run? I refuse! Ignore run My boss evil brave tells me pack, escape! Go! evil demon tells me I decide stay my mind , my heart wise, tells me

friend Launcelot, being an honest man's son' -- or rather 'an honest woman's son,' for indeed my father did something smack, something grow to; he had a kind of taste -- Well, my conscience says, 'Launcelot, budge not.' 'Budge,' says the fiend. 'Budge not,' says my conscience. 'Conscience,' say I, 'you counsel well.' 'Fiend,' say I, 'you counsel well.' To be ruled by my conscience, I should stay with the Jew my master who, God bless the mark, is a kind of devil; and to run away from the Jew, I should be ruled by the fiend who, saving your reverence, is the devil himself. Certainly the Jew is the very devil incarnation; And in my conscience, my conscience is but a kind of hard conscience to offer to counsel me to stay with the Jew. The fiend gives the more friendly counsel. I will run, fiend; my heels are at your commandment; I will run.	My honest friend, your father honest man, your mother honest woman To be true honest my father not honest he affairs had, anyway! My mind tells me Do not move MOVE! Demon yells I tell my mind, "mind you advise good. Demon you advise good too" Suppose I listen to mind result? I stay with boss, jew, himself idea same devil (cross yourself) Suppose I listen to demon result? I escape not right, but I not want stay with boss I believe boss jew idea same devil My mind, hard thinking thinking Advise I stay with jew boss Demon advise me more friendly I agree demon I will run!
Think about doing this as if you are physically being pulled between a devil on your shoulder and an angel on your shoulder	

ROMEO Romeo and Juliet Scene III

(photo: Jerald Greer at the NYC Deaf Theater Festival at IRT, photographer: Don Petit-Homme)

JULIET appears above at a window

But, soft! what light through yonder window breaks?
It is the east, and Juliet is the sun.
Arise, fair sun, and kill the envious moon,
Who is already sick and pale with grief,
That thou her maid art far more fair than she:
Be not her maid, since she is envious;
Her vestal livery is but sick and green
And none but fools do wear it; cast it off.
It is my lady, O, it is my love!
O, that she knew she were!
She speaks yet she says nothing: what of that?
Her eye discourses; I will answer it.
I am too bold, 'tis not to me she speaks:

Two of the fairest stars in all the heaven,
Having some business, do entreat her eyes
To twinkle in their spheres till they return.
What if her eyes were there, they in her head?
The brightness of her cheek would shame those stars,
As daylight doth a lamp; her eyes in heaven
Would through the airy region stream so bright
That birds would sing and think it were not night.
See, how she leans her cheek upon her hand!
O, that I were a glove upon that hand,
That I might touch that cheek!

ENGLSIH	ASL GLOSS
JULIET *appears above at a window*	(He sees Juliet in the window above him)
	Calm, quiet Window above light glows. That light idea same East sun rise
But, soft! what light through yonder window breaks? It is the east, and Juliet is the sun.	Juliet idea same sun.
	Come Juliet my sun kill moon light moon jealous of you. Moon white pale sick jealous compare to sun can't
Arise, fair sun, and kill the envious moon, Who is already sick and pale with grief,	Juliet my sun you serve moon but you more beautiful. Serve moon finish moon jealous of you.
That thou her maid art far more fair than she: Be not her maid, since she is envious; Her vestal livery is but sick and green	Moon make you dress sick green dark throw off ! Only fools wear moon
And none but fools do wear it; cast it off. It is my lady, O, it is my love! O, that she knew she were!	(Juliet is now looking out of the window) That Juliet, my lady, my love Oh!
She speaks yet she says nothing: what of that? Her eye discourses; I will answer it.	Oh I wish she know I love her She talks but I hear nothing not important
I am too bold, 'tis not to me she speaks: Two of the fairest stars in all the heaven,	Her eyes tell stories I will respond I hold tongue – she talks but not to me
Having some business, do entreat her eyes To twinkle in their spheres till they return.	Heaven two stars have - Juliet look at stars not me
What if her eyes were there, they in her head? The brightness of her cheek would shame those stars,	Her eyes like stars sparkle – I want her look-at me
As daylight doth a lamp; her eyes in heaven	If Juliet's eye true biz in sky same stars not succeed her cheek red bright embarrass them Make us think night finish
	Her eyes same as lamp, her eyes sparkle in

Would through the airy region stream so bright	heave same as stars. Her eyes so bright world
That birds would sing and think it were not	lights up birds misunderstand and sing think
night.	morning arrive
See, how she leans her cheek upon her hand!	(she leans out window)
O, that I were a glove upon that hand,	She lean hand on cheek
That I might touch that cheek!	I wish I replace hand
	I wish I touch her cheek can!

Midsummer Night's Dream by William Shakespeare

Oberon (King of the Faeries)

ENGLISH   WRITE YOUR TRANSLATION GLOSS HERE

I know a bank where the wild thyme blows,
Where oxlips and the nodding violet grows,
Quite over-canopied with luscious woodbine,
With sweet musk-roses and with eglantine:
There sleeps Titania sometime of the night,
Lull'd in these flowers with dances and delight;
And there the snake throws her enamell'd skin,
Weed wide enough to wrap a fairy in:
And with the juice of this I'll streak her eyes,
And make her full of hateful fantasies.
Take thou some of it, and seek through this grove:
A sweet Athenian lady is in love
With a disdainful youth: anoint his eyes;
But do it when the next thing he espies
May be the lady: thou shalt know the man
By the Athenian garments he hath on.
Effect it with some care, that he may prove
More fond on her than she upon her love:
And look thou meet me ere the first cock crow.

(Photo: Alex and Pierre Wess Donald Panara Stage.
Photographer: Erin Thomas)

Tartuffe

A monologue from the play by Molière

Madam, no happiness is so complete
As when, from lips we love, come words so sweet;
Their nectar floods my every sense, and drains
In honeyed rivulets through all my veins.
To please you is my joy; my only goal;
Your love is the restorer of my soul;
And yet I must beg leave, now, to confess
Some lingering doubts as to my happiness.
Might this not be a trick? Might not the catch
Be that you wish me to break off the match
With Marianne, and so have feigned to love me?
I shan't quite trust your fond opinion of me
Until the feelings you've expressed so sweetly
Are demonstrated somewhat more concretely.

ENGLISH	ASL GLOSS
Madam, no happiness is so complete As when, from lips we love, come words so sweet;	Woman fancy, my happy satisfied happen your lips speak sweet to me Your words sweet flows into my eyes flows

| Their nectar floods my every sense, and drains In honeyed rivulets through all my veins. To please you is my joy; my only goal; Your love is the restorer of my soul; And yet I must beg leave, now, to confess Some lingering doubts as to my happiness. Might this not be a trick? Might not the catch Be that you wish me to break off the match With Marianne, and so have feigned to love me? I shan't quite trust your fond opinion of me Until the feelings you've expressed so sweetly Are demonstrated somewhat more concretely. | through my whole body, blood becomes idea same honey. My life goal what? You happy, my only goal your happiness. Your love save my soul But I must beg permission to admit I have doubts about why I feel happy Maybe trick? Maybe you want me dis-connect my marriage with Marianne. Maybe you fake love trick me You tell me you strong positive opinion about me I not trust Your feelings you must show me proof clear! |

A MIDSUMMER NIGHT'S DREAM

A monologue from Act III, Scene ii

(photo: Cynobia Demps and Gabrielle Williams, as Puck IRT production, photographer, Luane Davis Haggerty)

by: William Shakespeare

PUCK: My mistress with a monster is in love.
Near to her close and consecrated bower,
While she was in her dull and sleeping hour,
A crew of patches, rude mechanicals,
That work for bread upon Athenian stalls,
Were met together to rehearse a play,
Intended for great Theseus' nuptial day.
The shallowest thickskin of that barren sort,
Who Pyramus presented in their sport,
Forsook his scene and entered in a brake.
When I did him at this advantage take,
An ass's nole I fixèd on his head.
Anon his Thisby must be answerèd,
And forth my mimic comes. When they him spy,
As wild geese that the creeping fowler eye,
Or russet-pated choughs, many in sort,
Rising and cawing at the gun's report,
Sever themselves and madly sweep the sky;
So at his sight away his fellows fly,
And at our stamp here o'er and o'er one falls;
He murder cries and help from Athens calls.
Their sense thus weak, lost with their fears thus strong,

Made senseless things begin to do them wrong,
For briers and thorns at their apparel snatch:
Some, sleeves -- some, hats; from yielders all things catch.
I led them on in this distracted fear
And left sweet Pyramus translated there,
When in that moment (so it came to pass)
Titania waked, and straightway loved an ass.

ENGLISH   ASL GLOSS

ENGLISH	ASL GLOSS
My mistress with a monster is in love.	Happen my boss fall –in-love monster
Near to her close and consecrated bower,	True biz happen close her bedroom
While she was in her dull and sleeping hour,	Happen she sleeping same time
A crew of patches, rude mechanicals,	Group big men tough working men try acting
That work for bread upon Athenian stalls,	come for for? rehearse play will perform
Were met together to rehearse a play,	Theseus wedding.
Intended for great Theseus' nuptial day.	Big Men practice story about Pyramus
The shallowest thickskin of that barren sort,	One very big man escape wander alone in
Who Pyramus presented in their sport,	forest
Forsook his scene and entered in a brake.	I grab magic spell and he become donkey –
When I did him at this advantage take,	head man
An ass's nole I fixèd on his head.	
Anon his Thisby must be answerèd,	He hear other actor call. He must say him line
And forth my mimic comes. When they him spy,	He enter rehearsal all big men look at him
	Freak out idea same birds happen hunter
As wild geese that the creeping fowler eye,	Gun shoots all birds fly fly
Or russet-pated choughs, many in sort,	Swirling fly and take off in sky
Rising and cawing at the gun's report,	
Sever themselves and madly sweep the sky;	Group big men pow out of there idea same
So at his sight away his fellows fly,	
And at our stamp here o'er and o'er one falls;	One man stamp feet
He murder cries and help from Athens calls.	One man yells murder, help from Athens
Their sense thus weak, lost with their fears thus strong,	They feel fear strong
Made senseless things begin to do them wrong,	They run not look, trip, fall bushes scratch,
For briers and thorns at their apparel snatch;	trees grab clothes, their sleeves, their hats
Some, sleeves -- some, hats; from yielders all things catch.	
	I chase make them run more
I led them on in this distracted fear	
And left sweet Pyramus translated there,	I left big man donkey-head man stay
When in that moment (so it came to pass)	Soon happen
Titania waked, and straightway loved an ass	My boss wake-up fall-in-love with donkey-head man look like ASS!

(Photo from NTID Drama Club production of "Trick of Treat" photographer: Luane Davis Haggerty)

**HAMLET Act III Scene I
By William Shakespeare**

ENGLISH

WRITE YOUR TRANSLATION
GLOSS HERE

Ham. To be, or not to be: that is the question:
Whether 'tis nobler in the mind to suffer
The slings and arrows of outrageous fortune,   *68*
Or to take arms against a sea of troubles,
And by opposing end them? To die: to sleep;
No more; and, by a sleep to say we end
The heart-ache and the thousand natural shocks   *72*
That flesh is heir to, 'tis a consummation
Devoutly to be wish'd. To die, to sleep;
To sleep: perchance to dream: ay, there's the rub;
For in that sleep of death what dreams may come   *76*
When we have shuffled off this mortal coil,
Must give us pause. There's the respect
That makes calamity of so long life;
For who would bear the whips and scorns of time,   *80*
The oppressor's wrong, the proud man's contumely,
The pangs of dispriz'd love, the law's delay,
The insolence of office, and the spurns
That patient merit of the unworthy takes,   *84*
When he himself might his quietus make
With a bare bodkin? who would fardels bear,
To grunt and sweat under a weary life,

But that the dread of something after death,   *88*
The undiscover'd country from whose bourn
No traveller returns, puzzles the will,
And makes us rather bear those ills we have
Than fly to others that we know not of?   *92*
Thus conscience does make cowards of us all;
And thus the native hue of resolution
Is sicklied o'er with the pale cast of thought,
And enterprises of great pith and moment   *96*
With this regard their currents turn awry,
And lose the name of action.

TAMING OF THE SHREW Act IV Scene I
By William Shakespeare

Role of Petruchio

(photo left: Dack Virning, photographer: Erin Thomas)

ENGLISH

WRITE YOUR TRANSLATION GLOSS HERE

Pet. Thus have I politicly begun my reign,
And 'tis my hope to end successfully.
My falcon now is sharp and passing empty,   *128*
And till she stoop she must not be full-gorg'd,
For then she never looks upon her lure.
Another way I have to man my haggard,
To make her come and know her keeper's call;   *132*
That is, to watch her, as we watch these kites
That bate and beat and will not be obedient.
She eat no meat to-day, nor none shall eat;

Last night she slept not, nor to-night she shall not: *136*
As with the meat, some undeserved fault
I'll find about the making of the bed;
And here I'll fling the pillow, there the bolster,
This way the coverlet, another way the sheets: *140*
Ay, and amid this hurly I intend
That all is done in reverend care of her;
And in conclusion she shall watch all night:
And if she chance to nod I'll rail and brawl,   *144*
And with the clamour keep her still awake.
This is a way to kill a wife with kindness;
And thus I'll curb her mad and headstrong humour.
He that knows better how to tame a shrew,   *148*
Now let him speak: 'tis charity to show. [*Exit.*

THE TEMPEST Act I Scene II
By William Shakespeare

Role of Caliban
(photo: Anita Kuran, photographer: Luane Davis
Haggerty)

Cal.   I must eat my dinner.
This island's mine, by Sycorax my mother,   *396*
Which thou tak'st from me. When thou camest first,
Thou strok'dst me, and mad'st much of me; wouldst give me
Water with berries in't; and teach me how
To name the bigger light, and how the less,   *400*
That burn by day and night: and then I lov'd thee
And show'd thee all the qualities o' th' isle,
The fresh springs, brine-pits, barren place, and fertile.

Cursed be I that did so!—All the charms

Of Sycorax, toads, beetles, bats, light on you!

For I am all the subjects that you have,

Which first was mine own king; and here you sty me

In this hard rock, whiles you do keep from me

The rest o' th' island.

Cal. I must eat my dinner.	Dinner I eat must
This island's mine, by Sycorax my mother,	Here island mine. My mother name what?
Which thou tak'st from me. When thou camest first,	Sycoras gave me island here
	You arrive you steal island from me
Thou strok'dst me, and mad'st much of me; wouldst give me	You trick me nice, flatter pat head then steal!
Water with berries in't; and teach me how	You feed me water mix with berries
To name the bigger light, and how the less,	You teach me name for sun and moon
That burn by day and night: and then I lov'd thee	Day and night I love you past
And show'd thee all the qualities o' th' isle,	I guide you show you all island
The fresh springs, brine-pits, barren place, and fertile.	Beautiful water, good land bad land I show all
Cursed be I that did so!—All the charms	Dam me I show you all
Of Sycorax, toads, beetles, bats, light on you!	I wish I magic skill same my mother Sycorax
For I am all the subjects that you have,	I magic frogs, bugs, bats all attack you
Which first was mine own king; and here you sty me	Now I your slave
	Past I king
In this hard rock, whiles you do keep from me	How I prisoner here on hard rock
The rest o' th' island.	You not allow me go to all my island.

THE TEMPEST Act VI Scene I
By William Shakespeare

Role of Ariel
(Photo: Della Gorelick, photographer; Erin Thomas)

Ari. I told you, sir, they were red-hot with drinking;
So full of valour that they smote the air
For breathing in their faces; beat the ground   188
For kissing of their feet; yet always bending
Towards their project. Then I beat my tabor;
At which, like unback'd colts, they prick'd their ears,
Advanc'd their eyelids, lifted up their noses   192
As they smelt music: so I charm'd their ears
That, calf-like, they my lowing follow'd through
Tooth'd briers, sharp furzes, pricking goss and thorns,
Which enter'd their frail shins: at last I left them   196
I' the filthy-mantled pool beyond your cell,
There dancing up to the chins, that the foul lake
O'erstunk their feet.

Ari. I told you, sir, they were red-hot with drinking;	I tell finish SIR
So full of valour that they smote the air	Two-men drunk finish
For breathing in their faces; beat the ground	They act brave fake fight hit nothing
For kissing of their feet; yet always bending	I blow on their face – they try fight earth
Towards their project. Then I beat my tabor;	I kiss their feet, they confused keep drinking
At which, like unback'd colts, they prick'd	I beat drum
	They idea same wild horse
	Ears point up

their ears,	
Advanc'd their eyelids, lifted up their noses	Big eyes look around, sniff air
As they smelt music: so I charm'd their ears	Silly they think they can smell my drum?
That, calf-like, they my lowing follow'd through	I magic spell their ears can hear me sing and follow me
Tooth'd briers, sharp furzes, pricking goss and thorns,	I lead through terrible places
	Bush with thorns, sticking seeds, sharp grasses
Which enter'd their frail shins: at last I left them	They shins scrape
I' the filthy-mantled pool beyond your cell,	I leave them where?
There dancing up to the chins, that the foul lake	In the dirty water pool behind your house
	They stay in dirty water dancing water up to chin
O'erstunk their feet.	Now they smell worse than stinky feet!

Macbeth Act II Scene I
By William Shakespeare

Role of Macbeth

(Photo on right NTID production of MacBeth, reprinted with permission from NTID Performing Arts archive)

Is this a dagger which I see before me,

The handle toward my hand? Come, let me clutch thee: 44

I have thee not, and yet I see thee still.

Art thou not, fatal vision, sensible

To feeling as to sight? or art thou but   48

A dagger of the mind, a false creation,

Proceeding from the heat-oppressed brain?

I see thee yet, in form as palpable

As this which now I draw.   52

Thou marshall'st me the way that I was going;

And such an instrument I was to use.

Mine eyes are made the fools o' the other senses,

Or else worth all the rest: I see thee still;   *56*

And on thy blade and dudgeon gouts of blood,

Which was not so before. There's no such thing:

It is the bloody business which informs

Thus to mine eyes   *60*

[*A bell rings.*   *72*

I go, and it is done; the bell invites me.

Hear it not, Duncan; for it is a knell

That summons thee to heaven or to hell. [*Exit.*

Is this a dagger which I see before me,	I dream I see knife in front of me I reach and knife in my hand
The handle toward my hand? Come, let me clutch thee:	I want hold knife but feel nothing
I have thee not, and yet I see thee still.	But in my dream knife is still there
Art thou not, fatal vision, sensible	My dream dangerous? Prophecy? Real fake which?
To feeling as to sight? or art thou but	
A dagger of the mind, a false creation,	Maybe a dream knife I make-up
Proceeding from the heat-oppressed brain?	My mind hot
I see thee yet, in form as palpable	Still I can imagine knife. It looks real same as
As this which now I draw.	(refer to knife you have on you)
Thou marshall'st me the way that I was going;	Knife lead me to goal
And such an instrument I was to use.	I plan use knife
Mine eyes are made the fools o' the other senses,	My eyes trick me I can se but can't touch
Or else worth all the rest: I see thee still;	My eyes tell truth better than other senses
And on thy blade and dudgeon gouts of blood,	I see knife covered in blood, dripping
Which was not so before. There's no such thing:	Before knife clean Not future see bloody, murder

It is the bloody business which informs	This tells me my future
Thus to mine eyes [*A bell rings.* I go, and it is done; the bell invites me.	My eyes, see (bell) Time go now, bell ring ring invites me go find Duncan
Hear it not, Duncan; for it is a knell	I think Duncan hear not.
That summons thee to heaven or to hell. [*Exit.*	That bell announces Duncan will die go heaven hell not important (Exit)

Othello Act II Scene I By William Shakespeare

Role of Iago

(Photo: Troy Chapman, Lou Labriola, photographer: Erin Thomas)

Iago. That Cassio loves her, I do well believe it;
That she loves him, 'tis apt, and of great credit:
The Moor, howbeit that I endure him not,
Is of a constant, loving, noble nature;   232
And I dare think he'll prove to Desdemona
A most dear husband. Now, I do love her too;
Not out of absolute lust,—though peradventure
I stand accountant for as great a sin,—   236
But partly led to diet my revenge,
For that I do suspect the lusty Moor
Hath leap'd into my seat; the thought whereof
Doth like a poisonous mineral gnaw my inwards;   240
And nothing can or shall content my soul
Till I am even'd with him, wife for wife;

Or failing so, yet that I put the Moor

At least into a jealousy so strong

That judgment cannot cure.

Iago. That Cassio loves her, I do well believe it;	Cassio fall-in-love Othello's wife I believe
That she loves him, 'tis apt, and of great credit:	Othello's wife love Cassio I doubt but two of them fit
The Moor, howbeit that I endure him not,	I hate Othello but he is good husband, love his wife, continues, brave, she love him too
Is of a constant, loving, noble nature;	
And I dare think he'll prove to Desdemona	I love Othello's wife too
A most dear husband. Now, I do love her too;	
Not out of absolute lust,—though peradventure	Not from attraction to her beauty
I stand accountant for as great a sin,—	Yes she is beautiful But I attracted to use Othello's wife to win revenge against Othello
But partly led to diet my revenge,	
For that I do suspect the lusty Moor	
Hath leap'd into my seat; the thought whereof	I think Othello jump into bed with my wife
Doth like a poisonous mineral gnaw my inwards;	I jealous think, thought eats my brain and my guts
And nothing can or shall content my soul	
Till I am even'd with him, wife for wife;	I upset nothing can calm me I want equal My wife equal his wife
Or failing so, yet that I put the Moor	If I can't make him doubt wife same as me
At least into a jealousy so strong	Then I make him jealous same as me
That judgment cannot cure.	He can't avoid awful thoughts

Men's Contemporary Monologues

EXTRACTS FROM ADAM'S DIARY
A monologue from the book by Mark Twain

NOTE: This monologue is reprinted from Extracts From Adam's Diary. Mark Twain. New York: Harper & Brothers, 1904.

(photo: Joseph Fox, photographer; Mark Benjamin)

Joseph Fox

ADAM: She has no discrimination. She takes to all the animals--all of them! She thinks they are all treasures, every new one is welcome. When the brontosaurus came striding into camp, she regarded it as an acquisition, I considered it a calamity; that is a good sample of the lack of harmony that prevails in our views of things. She wanted to domesticate it, I wanted to make it a present of the homestead and move out. She believed it could be tamed by kind treatment and would be a good pet; I said a pet twenty-one feet high and eighty-four feet long would be no proper thing to have about the place, because, even with the best intentions and without meaning any harm, it could sit down on the house and mash it, for any one could see by the look of its eye that it was absent-minded. Still, her heart was set upon having that monster, and she couldn't give it up. She thought we could start a dairy with it, and wanted me to help milk it; but I wouldn't; it was too risky. The sex wasn't right, and we hadn't any ladder anyway. Then she wanted to ride it, and look at the scenery. Thirty or forty feet of its tail was lying on the ground, like a fallen tree, and she thought she could climb it, but she was mistaken; when she got to the steep place it was too slick and down she came, and would have hurt herself but for me. Was she satisfied now? No. Nothing ever satisfies her but demonstration; untested theories are not in her line, and she won't have them. It is the right spirit, I concede it; it attracts me; I feel the influence of it; if I were with her more I think I should take it up myself. Well, she had one theory remaining about this colossus: she thought that if we could tame it and make him friendly we could stand in the river and use him for a bridge. It turned out that he was already plenty tame enough--at least as far as she was concerned--so she tried her theory, but it failed: every time she got him properly placed in the river and went ashore to cross over him, he came out and followed her around like a pet mountain. Like the other animals. They all do that.

She has no discrimination. She takes to all the animals--all of them! She thinks they are all treasures, every new one is welcome. When the brontosaurus came striding into camp, she regarded it as an acquisition, I considered it a calamity; that is a good sample of the lack of harmony that prevails in our views of things. She wanted to domesticate it, I wanted to make it a present of the homestead and move out.	Eve discrimination none. Eve herself likes all animals – ALL! She think all animals precious all are welcome. Happen dinosaur walk into house she think dinosaur is pet! She happy I think terrible Story example we not agree Eve want pet, I want run away
She believed it could be tamed by kind treatment and would be a good pet; I said a pet twenty-one feet high and eighty-four feet long would be no proper thing to have about the place, because, even with the best intentions and without meaning any harm, it could sit down on the house and mash it, for any one	Eve believe we can calm dinosaur. Feed it nice touch dinosaur good pet will I say NO! dinosaur tall 21 feet big 81 feet long Not right to keep, dinosaur destroy everything our house dinosaur sit on, crush Other people can understand Dinsosaur dumb

could see by the look of its eye that it was absent-minded. Still, her heart was set upon having that monster, and she couldn't give it up. She thought we could start a dairy with it, and wanted me to help milk it; but I wouldn't; it was too risky. The sex wasn't right, and we hadn't any ladder anyway. Then she wanted to ride it, and look at the scenery. Thirty or forty feet of its tail was lying on the ground, like a fallen tree, and she thought she could climb it, but she was mistaken; when she got to the steep place it was too slick and down she came, and would have hurt herself but for me. Was she satisfied now? No. Nothing ever satisfies her but demonstration; untested theories are not in her line, and she won't have them. It is the right spirit, I concede it; it attracts me; I feel the influence of it; if I were with her more I think I should take it up myself. Well, she had one theory remaining about this colossus: she thought that if we could tame it and make him friendly we could stand in the river and use him for a bridge. It turned out that he was already plenty tame enough--at least as far as she was concerned--so she tried her theory, but it failed: every time she got him properly placed in the river and went ashore to cross over him, he came out and followed her around like a pet mountain. Like the other animals. They all do that.	But Eve want dinosaur monster become pet, she not give up idea She think maybe we can milk it, she want me to help I refuse. I don't want risk

It not female dinosaur, I need ladder, don't want milk dinosaur. Then Eve want ride dinosaur look look.

She see tail tries to climb up but slips falls slides down, I catch Eve. If I not catch, she hurt herself.

Eve satisfied? No! She satisfied never, she want experiment, theory. I like her spirit she attracts me. She influence me. If two-of-us together I maybe agree with her and try to ride dinosaur myself.

Eve has one more idea for dinosaur – she think we calm dinosaur stand in river and he become bridge. She can use dinosaur to cross river but then dinosaur follow her like pet mountain and she can't come back. Dinosaur same all animal

All animals follow Eve. |

GETTING MARRIED
A monologue from the play by <u>George Bernard Shaw</u>

NOTE: This monologue is reprinted from <u>The Doctor's Dilemma, Getting Married, and The Shewing-Up of Blanco Posnet</u>. Bernard Shaw. New York: Brentano's, 1909.

(Photo: Anthony Russo, photographer: Mark Benjamin)

COLLINS: No, maam; marriage didn't come natural. My wife had to break me into it. It came natural to her: she's what you might call a regular old hen. Always wants to have her family within sight of her. Wouldn't go to bed unless she knew they was all safe at home and the door locked, and the lights out. Always wants her luggage in the carriage with her. Always goes and makes the engine driver promise her to be careful. She's a born wife and mother, maam. That's why my children all ran away from home. I very often felt inclined to run away myself, but when it came to the point I couldn't bear to hurt her feelings. She's a sensitive, affectionate, anxious soul; and she was never brought up to know what freedom is to some people. You see, family life is all the life she knows: she's like a bird born in a cage, that would die if you let it loose in the woods. When I thought how little it was to a man of my easy temper to put up with her, and how deep it would hurt her to think it was because I didn't care for her, I always put off running away till next time; and so in the end I never ran away at all. I daresay it was good for me to be took such care of; but it cut me off from all my old friends something dreadful, maam: especially the women, maam. She never gave them a chance; she didn't indeed. She never understood that married people should take holidays from one another if they are to keep at all fresh. Not that I ever got tired of her, maam; but my! how I used to get tired of home life sometimes. I used to catch myself envying my brother George: I positively did,

Anthony Russo

maam. He married a very fine figure of a woman; but she was that changeable and what you might call susceptible, you would not believe. She didn't seem to have any control over herself when she fell in love. She would mope for a couple of days, crying about nothing; and then she would up and say--no matter who was there to hear her--"I must go to him, George!"; and away she would go from her home and her husband without with-your-leave or by-your-leave.

ENGLISH	WRITE YOUR TRANSLATION GLOSS HERE
No, maam; marriage didn't come natural. My wife had to break me into it. It came natural to her: she's what you might call a regular old hen. Always wants to have her family within sight of her. Wouldn't go to bed unless she knew they was all safe at home and the door locked, and the lights out. Always wants her luggage in the carriage with her. Always goes and makes the engine driver promise her to be careful. She's a born wife and mother, maam. That's why my children all ran away from home. I very often felt inclined to run away myself, but when it came to the point I couldn't bear to hurt her feelings. She's a sensitive, affectionate, anxious soul; and she was never brought up to know what freedom is to some people. You see, family life is all the life she knows: she's like a bird born in a cage, that would die if you let it loose in the woods. When I thought how little it was to a man of my easy temper to put up with her, and how deep it would hurt her to think it was because I	No ma'am (woman) marriage easy not natural not. My wife train me.

My wife think marriage easy she idea same old chicken – means she always wants family close. Happen night she wait all safe, door locked, lights out then can sleep. Happen she travel bag must stay with her not travel separate from bag. Happen on train travel she asks driver you be safe!

My wife idea same born wife/mother. That's why all our children escape home. Sometimes I want escape home same but don't want hurt wife's feelings. My wife sensitive, sweet easy worry soul. She not understand "freedom". She only know family life idea same bird in cage. Suppose you let bird out of cage to live in forest, happen bird die will.

Easy for me to accept my wife her ways – not want hurt her, don't want her think I stop love |

didn't care for her, I always put off running away till next time; and so in the end I never ran away at all. I daresay it was good for me to be took such care of; but it cut me off from all my old friends something dreadful, maam: especially the women, maam. She never gave them a chance; she didn't indeed. She never understood that married people should take holidays from one another if they are to keep at all fresh. Not that I ever got tired of her, maam; but my! how I used to get tired of home life sometimes. I used to catch myself envying my brother George: I positively did, maam. He married a very fine figure of a woman; but she was that changeable and what you might call susceptible, you would not believe. She didn't seem to have any control over herself when she fell in love. She would mope for a couple of days, crying about nothing; and then she would up and say--no matter who was there to hear her--"I must go to him, George!"; and away she would go from her home and her husband without with-your-leave or by-your-leave.	her. Postpone escape wait for next time, result I never run away. My wife takes care me well, but means my old friends disconnect. Terrible "maam" Speial women "maam" My wife never liked my women friends, never understood married people can vacation separate then when together feels new. I'm not say I tired bored with wife no ma'am But sometimes I jealous my brother George. George, his wife nice shape but she change her mind always. Seems no control happen she fall-in-love. First she sad few days, cry about nothing, next she say "I go to new love George" and she leave home, husband everything, never ask permission!

MOBY DICK
A monologue from the novel by Herman Melville

> NOTE: This monologue is reprinted from Moby Dick; or, the Whale.
> Herman Melville. New York: Harper & Brothers, 1851.

(Photo: Mir Ayaz Ali, photographer: Mark Benjamin)

Ayaz Ali

STUBB: Such a queer dream, King-Post, I never had. You know the old man's ivory leg, well I dreamed he kicked me with it; and when I tried to kick back, upon my soul, my little man, I kicked my leg right off! And then, presto! Ahab seemed a pyramid, and I, like a blazing fool, kept kicking at it. But what was still more curious, Flask--you know how curious all dreams are--through all this rage that I was in, I somehow seemed to be thinking to myself, that after all, it was not much of an insult, that kick from Ahab. 'Why,' thinks I, 'what's the row? It's not a real leg, only a false leg.' And there's a mighty difference between a living thump and a dead thump. That's what makes a blow from the hand, Flask, fifty times more savage to bear than a blow from a cane. The living member--that makes the living insult, my little man. And thinks I to myself all the while, mind, while I was stubbing my silly toes against that cursed pyramid--so confoundedly contradictory was it all, all the while, I say, I was thinking to myself, 'what's his leg now, but a cane--a whalebone cane. Yes,' thinks I, 'it was only a playful cudgelling--in fact, only a whaleboning that he gave me--not a base kick. Captain Ahab kicked me, didn't he?' 'Yes, he did,' says I--'right HERE it was.' He used his ivory leg, didn't he?' 'Yes, he did,' . 'Well then,I says to myself 'wise Stubb, what have you to complain of? Didn't he kick with right good will? it wasn't a common pitch pine leg he kicked with, was it? No, you were kicked by a great man, and with a beautiful ivory leg, Stubb. It's an honour; I consider it an honour. Listen, wise Stubb. In old England the greatest lords think it great glory to be slapped by a queen, and made garter-knights of; but, be YOUR boast, Stubb, that ye were kicked by old Ahab, and made a wise man of. Remember what I say; BE kicked by him; account his kicks honours; and on no account kick back; for you can't help yourself, wise Stubb. Don't you see that pyramid?' With that, he all of a sudden seemed somehow, in some queer fashion, to swim off into the air. I snored; rolled over; and there I was in my hammock! Now, what do you think of that dream, Flask?

ENGLISH   WRITE YOUR TRANSLATION GLOSS HERE

Such a queer dream, King-Post, I never had. You know the old man's ivory leg, well I dreamed he kicked me with it; and when I tried to kick back, upon my soul, my little man, I kicked my leg right off! And then, presto! Ahab seemed a pyramid, and I, like a blazing fool, kept kicking at it. But what was still more curious, Flask--you know how curious all dreams are--through all this rage that I was in, I somehow seemed to be thinking to myself, that after all, it was not much of an insult, that kick from Ahab. 'Why,' thinks I, 'what's the row? It's not a real leg, only a false leg.' And there's a mighty difference between a living thump and a dead thump. That's what makes a blow from the hand, Flask, fifty times more savage to bear than a blow from a cane. The living member-- that makes the living insult, my little man. And thinks I to myself all the while, mind, while I was stubbing my silly toes against that cursed pyramid--so confoundedly contradictory was it all, all the while, I say, I was thinking to myself, 'what's his leg now, but a cane--a whalebone cane. Yes,' thinks I, 'it was only a playful cudgelling--in fact, only a whaleboning that he gave me--not a base kick. Captain Ahab kicked me, didn't he?' 'Yes, he did,' says I-- 'right HERE it was.' He used his ivory leg, didn't he?' 'Yes, he did,' . 'Well then,I says to	

myself 'wise Stubb, what have you to complain of? Didn't he kick with right good will? it wasn't a common pitch pine leg he kicked with, was it? No, you were kicked by a great man, and with a beautiful ivory leg, Stubb. It's an honour; I consider it an honour. Listen, wise Stubb. In old England the greatest lords think it great glory to be slapped by a queen, and made garter-knights of; but, be YOUR boast, Stubb, that ye were kicked by old Ahab, and made a wise man of. Remember what I say; BE kicked by him; account his kicks honours; and on no account kick back; for you can't help yourself, wise Stubb. Don't you see that pyramid?' With that, he all of a sudden seemed somehow, in some queer fashion, to swim off into the air. I snored; rolled over; and there I was in my hammock! Now, what do you think of that dream, Flask?

THE BOOR
A monologue from the play by Anton Chekhov

NOTE: This monologue is reprinted from Contemporary One-Act Plays. Ed. Lewis, B. Roland. New York: Charles Scribner's Sons, 1922.

(Photo: J.W. Guido, photographer: Mark Benjamin)

SMIRNOV: I don't understand how to behave in the company of ladies. Madam, in the course of my life I have seen more women than you have sparrows. Three times have I fought duels for women, twelve I jilted and nine jilted me. There was a time when I played the fool, used honeyed language, bowed and scraped. I loved, suffered, sighed to the moon, melted in love's torments. I loved passionately, I loved to madness, loved in every key, chattered like a magpie on emancipation, sacrificed half my fortune in the tender passion, until now the devil knows I've had enough of it. Your obedient servant will let you lead him around by the nose no more. Enough! Black eyes, passionate eyes, coral lips, dimples in cheeks, moonlight whispers, soft, modest sights-- for all that, madam, I wouldn't pay a kopeck! I am not speaking of present company, but of women in general; from the tiniest to the greatest, they are conceited, hypocritical, chattering, odious, deceitful from top to toe; vain, petty, cruel with a maddening logic and in this respect, please excuse my frankness, but one sparrow is worth

JW Guido

ten of the aforementioned petticoat-philosophers. When one sees one of the romantic creatures before him he imagines he is looking at some holy being, so wonderful that its one breath could dissolve him in a sea of a thousand charms and delights; but if one looks into the soul--it's nothing but a common crocodile. But the worst of all is that this crocodile imagines it is a masterpiece of creation, and that it has a monopoly on all the tender passions. May the devil hang me upside down if there is anything to love about a woman! When she is in love, all she knows is how to complain and shed tears. If the man suffers and makes sacrifices she swings her train about and tries to lead him by the nose. You have the misfortune to be a woman, and naturally you know woman's nature; tell me on your honor, have you ever in your life seen a woman who was really true and faithful? Never! Only the old and the deformed are true and faithful. It's easier to find a cat with horns or a white woodcock, than a faithful woman.

ENGLISH	WRITE YOUR TRANSLATION GLOSS HERE
I don't understand how to behave in the company of ladies. Madam, in the course of my life I have seen more women than you have sparrows. Three times have I fought duels for women, twelve I jilted and nine jilted me. There was a time when I played the fool, used honeyed language, bowed and scraped. I loved, suffered, sighed to the moon, melted in love's torments. I loved passionately, I loved to madness, loved in every key, chattered like a magpie on emancipation, sacrificed half my fortune in the tender passion, until now the devil knows I've had enough of it. Your obedient servant will let you lead him around by the nose no more. Enough! Black eyes, passionate eyes, coral lips, dimples in cheeks, moonlight whispers, soft, modest sights--for all that, madam, I wouldn't pay a kopeck! I am not speaking of present company, but of women in general; from the tiniest to the greatest, they are conceited, hypocritical, chattering, odious, deceitful from top to toe; vain, petty, cruel with a maddening logic and in this respect, please excuse my frankness, but one sparrow is worth ten of the aforementioned petticoat-philosophers. When one sees one of the romantic creatures before him he imagines he is looking at some holy being, so wonderful that its one breath could dissolve him in a sea of a thousand charms and delights; but if one looks into the soul--it's nothing but a common crocodile. But the worst of all is that this	

crocodile imagines it is a masterpiece of creation, and that it has a monopoly on all the tender passions. May the devil hang me upside down if there is anything to love about a woman! When she is in love, all she knows is how to complain and shed tears. If the man suffers and makes sacrifices she swings her train about and tries to lead him by the nose. You have the misfortune to be a woman, and naturally you know woman's nature; tell me on your honor, have you ever in your life seen a woman who was really true and faithful? Never! Only the old and the deformed are true and faithful. It's easier to find a cat with horns or a white woodcock, than a faithful woman.

THE GILDED AGE
A monologue from the book by Mark Twain

NOTE: This monologue is reprinted from The Gilded Age. Mark Twain. Hartford: American Publishing Co., 1873.

(photo: Kevin Reyes, photographer: Mark Benjamin)

SI HAWKINS: Wait, Nancy, wait--let me finish-- *[He drops his voice to a whisper and looks anxiously around to see that there are no eavesdroppers,]* --a thousand dollars an acre! Well you may open your eyes and stare! But it's so. You and I may not see the day, but they'll see it. Our children will see it! Mind I tell you; they'll see it. I've been watching--I've been watching while some people slept, and I know what's coming. Even you and I will see the day that steamboats will come up that little Turkey river to within twenty miles of this land of ours--and in high water they'll come right to it! And this is not all, Nancy--it isn't even half! There's a bigger wonder--the railroad! These worms here have never even heard of it--and when they do they'll not believe in it. But it's another fact. Coaches that fly over the ground twenty miles an hour--heavens and earth, think of that, Nancy! Twenty miles an hour. It makes a main's brain whirl. Some day, when you and I are in our graves, there'll be a railroad stretching hundreds of miles--all the way down from the cities of the Northern States to New Orleans--and its got to run within thirty miles of this land--may be even touch a corner of it. Well; do you know, they've quit burning wood in some places in the Eastern States? And what do you suppose they burn? Coal! There's worlds of it on this land! You know that black stuff that crops out of the bank of

Kevin Reyes

the branch?--well, that's it. You've taken it for rocks; so has every body here; and they've built little dams and such things with it. One man was going to build a chimney out of it. Nancy I expect I turned as white as a sheet! Why, it might have caught fire and told everything. I showed him it was too crumbly. Then he was going to build it of copper ore--splendid yellow forty-per-cent. ore! There's fortunes upon fortunes of copper ore on our land!

ENGLISH	WRITE YOUR TRANSLATION GLOSS HERE
Wait, Nancy, wait--let me finish-- *[He drops his voice to a whisper and looks anxiously around to see that there are no eavesdroppers,]* --a thousand dollars an acre! Well you may open your eyes and stare! But it's so. You and I may not see the day, but they'll see it. Our children will see it! Mind I tell you; they'll see it. I've been watching--I've been watching while some people slept, and I know what's coming. Even you and I will see the day that steamboats will come up that little Turkey river to within twenty miles of this land of ours--and in high water they'll come right to it! And this is not all, Nancy--it isn't even half! There's a bigger wonder--the railroad! These worms here have never even heard of it--and when they do they'll not believe in it. But it's another fact. Coaches that fly over the ground twenty miles an hour--heavens and earth, think of that, Nancy! Twenty miles an hour. It makes a main's brain whirl. Some day, when you and I are in our graves, there'll be a railroad stretching hundreds of miles--all the way down from the cities of the Northern States to New Orleans--and its got to run within thirty miles of this land--may be even touch a corner of it. Well; do you know, they've quit burning wood in some places in the Eastern States? And what do you suppose they burn? Coal! There's worlds of it on this land! You know that black stuff that crops out of the bank of the branch?--well, that's it. You've taken it for rocks; so has every body here; and they've built little dams and such things with it. One man was going to build a chimney out of it. Nancy I expect I turned as white as a sheet! Why, it might have caught fire and told everything. I showed him it was too crumbly. Then he was going to build	

it of copper ore--splendid yellow forty-per-cent. ore! There's fortunes upon fortunes of copper ore on our land!	

Women's Contemporary Monologues
A Raisin in the Sun
by Lorraine Hansberry

Role Lena Younger, she is talking to her son about the values of their family

Oh – so now it's life. Money is life? Once upon a time freedom used to be life. But now it's money. I guess the world really do change. No…Something has changed. You something new, boy. In my time, we was worried about not being lynched and getting to the North if we could and how to stay alive and still have dignity too. Now here come you and Beneatha talkin' 'bout things we ain't never even thought about, hardly, me and your Daddy. You ain't satisfied or proud of nothing we done. I mean, that you had a home; that we kept you out of trouble 'til you was grown; that you don't have to ride to work on the back of nobody's streetcar. You my children, but how different we've become.

Oh – so now it's life. Money is life? Once upon a time freedom used to be life. But now it's money. I guess the world really do change. No…Something has changed. You something new, boy. In my time, we was worried about not being lynched and getting to the North if we could and how to stay alive and still have dignity too. Now here come you and Beneatha talkin' 'bout things we ain't never even thought about, hardly, me and your Daddy. You ain't satisfied or proud of nothing we done. I mean, that you had a home; that we kept you out of trouble 'til you was grown; that you don't have to ride to work on the back of nobody's streetcar. You my children, but how different we've become.	Oh-I-See money equal life. Money equals life. Past freedom equal life but now change to money. I suppose the world true biz change. No me wrong something changed. You different kind of man. My past we worried white man catch us hang us with rope from tree. My past we worried we travel safe to north, stay alive, keep our pride. Now you and your sister Berneatha talk talk about things me your Dad never thought about. Seems you not proud, not satisfied you not feel proud my work your Dad's work. Pay attention you had a home, you not have trouble since you gre up. You not have to ride to work back of bus. Yes, two-of-you my children but grow up different than me

(Photo above: Antilla Zukifl plays Lena at the NYC Deaf Fest Photo next page: Don Petit-Homme and Martina Bell at NYC Deaf Fest performance of Raisin in the Sun, photographer: Luane Davis Haggerty)

Role of Beneatha
Talking to her Mother about her college life.

What are you talking about, "Get over it"? I'm going to be a doctor. I'm not even worried about who I'm going to marry yet. **If** I ever get married. (mother looks shocked and she reassures her) I probably will. But first I'm going to be a doctor. Now George, for one, thinks that's pretty funny. I couldn't be bothered with that. I'm going to be a doctor. And everybody here better understand that.And don't say "God willing" You don't understand. It's all a matter of ideas. And God is just one idea that I don't accept. Now it's not important. I'm not going to be immoral ...or commit crimes because I don't believe. I don't even think about that. I just get so tired of Him getting the credit for things the human race achieves through its own effort. Now, there simply is no God. There's only man. And it's he who makes miracles.

What are you talking about, "Get over it"? I'm going to be a doctor. I'm not even worried about who I'm going to marry yet. **If** I ever get married. (mother looks shocked and she reassures her) I probably will. But first I'm going to be a doctor. Now George, for one, thinks that's pretty funny. I couldn't be bothered with that. I'm going to be a doctor. And everybody here better understand that. And don't say "God willing" You don't understand. It's all a matter of ideas. And God is just one idea that I don't accept. Now it's not important. I'm not going to be immoral ...or commit crimes because I don't believe. I don't even think about that. I just get so tired of Him getting the credit for things the human race achieves through its own effort. Now, there simply is no God. There's only man. And it's he who makes miracles.	Don't understand you say accept it? No! My goal I want become doctor. I not think about marry someone IF I decide marry someone (mother shocked she reassures) I maybe marry future will but first I want become doctor. Boyfriend named George, he think my goal silly. Don't care I stubborn goal doctor. Everyone must understand me not say "God willing" NO! You don't understand. Poitn what? Ideas God is not idea I accept – not important not mean I bad or willing to steal break law no. I don't believe God real not mean I bad person. I tired God always positive positive credit. I feel human people succeed because work hard. There is no God There is only man Miracles? Only man make.

AUDITION
By Mathew Calhoun (reprinted with permission of the author)

(photo: Beth Applebaum, photographer: Mark Benjamin)
This comic monologue is printed here in its entirety, though written for a male actor, by changing a few pronouns, the piece could be adapted for use by an actress.

(An actor carrying an umbrella, enters. He/she is unusual looking in some ways... something different. He speaks forward to the audience, which represents the two or three people auditioning him Photo on left is Jerald Greer at the NYC Deaf Fest, photographer: Don Petit-Homme.)

Actor: My resume. *(He takes out a three-by-five card, and spins it forward, of the front of the stage.)* Oh, first I should mention that I could play any of the parts in this play. Any. I could play an ant, I could play Little Red Riding Hood, I could play Hamlet. I've never heard of this play, as a matter of fact. It doesn't matter. I can do opera, I can do commercials, I can sing soprano, I can do my own stunts- I'm that versatile. Leading man, leading lady, gay, ingenue- you name it, I can do it. That's how great I am. I see you looking over my resume. Noticing I've never had a part. It's a real comment on this sick business we're in, isn't it? An actor this good *(he thumps his chest)* and he's blackballed! Why? For refusing to show up at auditions! Auditions are beneath me. I wipe my feet on them. People should be begging me to grace their theatres- producers should be asking me to audition them! But those egomaniacs who should bow and scrape before me - they have forced me to betray my principles and come to this *(said with utter contempt)* audition. *(the word is practically spat, or vomited out. The contempt with which the actor feels this word is the key of the scene.)*

Beth Applebaum

So no, no, don't blame me for demeaning myself in this grotesque position... I've waited ten years for them to come crawling... but suffice it to say they were too wrapped up in their own insane... trivium to get the hint. But enough of them. Let's get to the situation at hand. You're sitting there typecasting me as a leading man aren't you? You're thinking that because of my matinee idol glorious good looks, and rich, sensuous, sexy, seductive, fetching, effervescent, tingly and charming voice, I could only play a male lead. No, I tell you, no! Observe! An ant! *(He crawls along the floor in a normal way.)* And now, King Lear! *(He opens his umbrella and pretends, in an awkward mime, to be blown around the stage.)* I needn't mention, of course, that that was the fabulous storm scene, out on the heath. And now, Brutus, impaled on his own sword! *(Closes the umbrella, stabs himself with it in the stomach. Dies, rather flatly.)*

And here's a homicidal lunatic: *(he gets up, picks up the umbrella, waves it threatening forward, like a sword. This part seems real.)* Give me the part or I'll kill you! I'll poke out the vile grape jelly of your eyes with the point of my umbrella! I've been waiting ten years for this! *(Puts the umbrella down.)*

OK. All the parts. I should play *all* the parts in you little production. Capiche? Capiche. Note the mastery of the Spanish dialect. I do it all. Now, with that in mind, here's my... *(Abrupt pause)*

What do you mean my time's up? I haven't done my monologue yet! *(Beat)* What do you mean, next? Where do *you* get off saying next?! I memorized this thing! I took the subway here! I elbowed my way ahead of dozens of pushy actors and still had to wait a half hour to get in here! I *wanna* do my audition!

ENGLISH	WRITE YOUR TRANSLATION HERE
My resume. *(He takes out a three-by-five card, and spins it forward, of the front of the stage.)* Oh, first I should mention that I could play any of the parts in this play. Any. I could play an ant, I could play Little Red Riding Hood, I could play Hamlet. I've never	

heard of this play, as a matter of fact. It doesn't matter. I can do opera, I can do commercials, I can sing soprano, I can do my own stunts- I'm that versatile. Leading man, leading lady, gay, ingenue- you name it, I can do it. That's how great I am. I see you looking over my resume. Noticing I've never had a part. It's a real comment on this sick business we're in, isn't it? An actor this good (*he thumps his chest*) and he's blackballed! Why? For refusing to show up at auditions! Auditions are beneath me. I wipe my feet on them. People should be begging me to grace their theatres- producers should be asking me to audition them! But those egomaniacs who should bow and scrape before me - they have forced me to betray my principles and come to this (*said with utter contempt*) audition. (*the word is practically spat, or vomited out. The contempt with which the actor feels this word is the key of the scene.*)

So no, no, don't blame me for demeaning myself in this grotesque position... I've waited ten years for them to come crawling... but suffice it to say they were too wrapped up in their own insane... trivium to get the hint. But enough of them. Let's get to the situation at hand. You're sitting there typecasting me as a leading man aren't you? You're thinking that because of my matinee idol glorious good looks, and rich, sensuous, sexy, seductive, fetching, effervescent, tingly and charming voice, I could only play a male lead. No, I tell you, no! Observe! An ant! (*He crawls along the floor in a normal way.*) And now, King Lear! (*He opens his umbrella and pretends, in an awkward mime, to be blown around the stage.*) I needn't mention, of course, that that was the fabulous storm scene, out on the heath. And now, Brutus, impaled on his own sword! (*Closes the umbrella, stabs himself with it in the stomach. Dies, rather flatly.*)

And here's a homicidal lunatic: (*he gets up, picks up the umbrella, waves it threatening forward, like a sword. This part seems real.*) Give me the part or I'll kill you! I'll poke out the vile grape jelly of your eyes with the point of my umbrella! I've been waiting ten years for this! (*Puts the umbrella down.*)

OK. All the parts. I should play *all* the parts in you little production. Capiche? Capiche. Note the mastery of the Spanish dialect. I do it all. Now, with that in mind, here's my... (*Abrupt pause*)

What do you mean my time's up? I haven't done my monologue yet! (*Beat*) What do you mean, next? Where do *you* get off saying next?! I memorized this thing! I took the subway here! I elbowed my way ahead of dozens of pushy actors and still had to wait a half hour to get in here! I *wanna* do my audition!

Nuts
by Tom Topor

Background Info: Claudia has been arrested on manslaughter charges. But before her trial, the prosecuting attorney requires she undergo psychiatric examination to see if she is able to stand trial. Claudia and her lawyer counter sue, and in this scene, is grilled by the prosecuting attorney on whether or not she is "nuts". She does very well, and just previous to this monologue, the prosecutor has just asked Claudia if she loves her mother.

When I was a little girl, I used to say to her, I love you to the moon and down again, and around the world and back again; and she used to say to me, I love you to the sun and down again, and around the stars and back again. Do you remember, Mama? And I used to think, wow, I love Mama and Mama loves me, and what can go wrong? What went wrong, Mama? I love you and you love me, and what went wrong? You see, I know she loves me, and I know I love her, and- so what? So what? She's over there, and I'm over here, and she hates me because of things I've done to her, and I hate her because of things she's done to me. You stand up there asking, do you love you daughter, and they say "yes", and you think you've asked something real, and they think they've said something real. You think because you throw the word love around like a frisbee that we're all going to get warm and runny. No. Something happens to some people. They love you so much, they stop noticing you're there, because they're so busy loving you. They love you so much, their love is a gun, and they fire it straight into your head. They love you so much you go right into the hospital. Yes, I know my mother loves me. Mama, I know you love me. And I know the one thing you learn when you grow up is that love is not enough. It's too much, and it's not enough.

When I was a little girl, I used to say to her, I love you to the moon and down again, and around the world and back again; and she used to say to me, I love you to the sun and down again, and around the stars and back again. Do you remember, Mama? And I used to think, wow, I love Mama and Mama loves me, and what can go wrong? What went wrong, Mama? I love you and you love me, and what went wrong? You see, I know she loves me, and I know I love her, and- so what? So what? She's over there, and I'm over here, and she hates me because of things I've done to her, and I hate her because of things she's done to me. You stand up there asking, do you love you daughter, and they say "yes", and you think you've asked something real, and they think they've said something real. You think because you throw the word love around like a frisbee that we're all going to get warm and runny. No. Something happens to some people. They love you so much, they stop noticing you're there, because they're so busy loving you. They love you so much, their love is a gun, and they fire it straight into your head. They love you so much you go right into the hospital. Yes, I know my mother loves me. Mama, I know you love me. And I know the one thing you learn when you grow up is that love is not enough. It's too much, and it's not enough	Happen past I little girl, I love my Mother Past I tell her my love big same as go to moon and stars and back. Mother past tell me my love big same as go to sun and stars travel around and around and back. You remember same? I remember I think WOW, mother loves me/I love mother wrong happen what? Wrong Mother? Understand, I know Mother loves me and I know I love her. Why important? Important because she sit far and I sit here, mother hates me because I hurt her. I hate her because she hurt me. You stand front of me ask me "so you love your daughter?" Mother says "yes" you think you have good questions, real question. You think throw word LOVE idea same Frisbee we all stop anger become warm happy. No! Some people change some people stop pay attention. Yes, love you but too busy to help you. Some people use love same gun shoot straight into head. Some people love so much force you go to hospital. Yes. I know my mother loves me. (looks at mother across room) Mother I know you love me. I also know now I become adult, love is not enough. Too much and not enough same time

Six Characters in Search of an Author
By Luigi Pirandello

The Step-Daughter: (stops, bends over the child and takes the latter's face between her hands) My little darling! You're frightened aren't you? You don't know where we are, do you? What is the stage? It s a place, baby, you know, where people play at being serious, a place where they act comedies. We've got to act a comedy now, dead serious, you know; and you're in it also, little one. (Embraces her, pressing the little head to her breast, and rocking the child for a moment) Oh darling, darling, what a horrid comedy you've got to play! What a wretched part they've found for you! A garden... a fountain... look... just suppose, kiddie, it's here. Where, you say? Why, right here in the middle. It's all pretence you know. That's the trouble, my pet: it's all make-believe here. It's better to imagine it though, because if they fix it up for you, it'll only be painted cardboard, painted cardboard for the rockery, the water, the plants... ah, but I think a baby like this one would sooner have a make believe fountain than a real one, so she could play with it. What a joke it'll be for the others! But for you, alas! Not quite such a joke: you who are real, baby dear and really play by a real fountain that is big and green and beautiful, with ever so many bamboos around it that are reflected in the water, and a whole lot of little ducks swimming about...

The Step-Daughter: (stops, bends over the child and takes the latter's face between her hands) My little darling! You're frightened aren't you? You don't know where we are, do you? What is the stage? It s a place, baby, you know, where people play at being serious, a place where they act comedies. We've got to act a comedy now, dead serious, you know; and you're in it also, little one. (Embraces her, pressing the little head to her breast, and rocking the child for a moment) Oh darling, darling, what a horrid comedy you've got to play! What a wretched part they've found for you! A garden... a fountain... look... just suppose, kiddie, it's here. Where, you say? Why, right here in the middle. It's all pretence you know. That's the trouble, my pet: it's all make-believe here. It's better to imagine it though, because if they fix it up for you, it'll only be painted cardboard, painted cardboard for the rockery, the water, the plants... ah, but I think a baby like this one would sooner have a make believe fountain than a real one, so she could play with it. What a joke it'll be for the others! But for you, alas! Not quite such a joke: you who are real, baby dear and really	You sweet! I scare you? Where? You don't know right? This is stage, what that? STAGE location happen people act seems serious or act funny. Now two-of-us will act funny, I serious, you in comedy with us little sweetie (hug child) Oh Sweet, sweet what a horrible comedy you have to act. Assign you awful role. Imagine garden here, a fountain ... Imagine you/me in garden with fountain, you ask me where? (mime it show her where) You imagine nothing real here everything is fake invent. Best way? Imagine then set people built it for you – not real life no – fake cardboard, paint not real. But you prefer fake you not want real right sweet? You want play play right? Other kids think this place a joke. But you know joke not. You are real, true biz baby sweet you go imagine better than real life... So you can play in a garden near a fountain can

play by a real fountain that is big and green and beautiful, with ever so many bamboos around it that are reflected in the water, and a whole lot of little ducks swimming about…	you see everything big green beautiful. Trees around water reflect trees. Can you dream, many ducks all swim in fountain … dream it

AN IDEAL HUSBAND
A monologue from the play by Oscar Wilde

> NOTE: This monologue is reprinted from An Ideal Husband. Oscar Wilde. London: Leonard Smithers, 1899.

(photo: Martina Bell, Beth Applebaum, Lauren Aggen, photographer: Amanda Stuhler)

MABEL CHILTERN: Well, Tommy has proposed to me again. Tommy really does nothing but propose to me. He proposed to me last night in the music-room, when I was quite unprotected, as there was an elaborate trio going on. I didn't dare to make the smallest repartee, I need hardly tell you. If I had, it would have stopped the music at once. Musical people are so absurdly unreasonable. They always want one to be perfectly dumb at the very moment when one is longing to be absolutely deaf. Then he proposed to me in broad daylight this morning, in front of that dreadful statue of Achilles. Really, the things that go on in front of that work of art are quite appalling. The police should interfere. At luncheon I saw by the glare in his eye that he was going to propose again, and I just managed to check him in time by assuring him that I was a bimetallist. Fortunately I don't know what bimetallism means. And I don't believe anybody else does either. But the observation crushed Tommy for ten minutes. He looked quite shocked. And then Tommy is so annoying in the way he proposes. If he proposed at the top of his voice, I should not mind so much. That might produce some effect on the public. But he does it in a horrid confidential way. When Tommy wants to be romantic he talks to one just like a doctor. I am very fond of Tommy, but his methods of proposing are quite out of date. I wish, Gertrude, you would speak to him, and tell him that once a week is quite often enough to propose to any one, and that it should always be done in a manner that attracts some attention.

ENGISH   WRITE YOUR TRANSLATION GLOSS HERE

Well, Tommy has proposed to me again. Tommy really does nothing but propose to me. He proposed to me last night in the music-room, when I was quite unprotected, as there was an elaborate trio going on. I didn't dare to make the smallest repartee, I need hardly tell you. If I had, it would have stopped the music	

at once. Musical people are so absurdly unreasonable. They always want one to be perfectly dumb at the very moment when one is longing to be absolutely deaf. Then he proposed to me in broad daylight this morning, in front of that dreadful statue of Achilles. Really, the things that go on in front of that work of art are quite appalling. The police should interfere. At luncheon I saw by the glare in his eye that he was going to propose again, and I just managed to check him in time by assuring him that I was a bimetallist. Fortunately I don't know what bimetallism means. And I don't believe anybody else does either. But the observation crushed Tommy for ten minutes. He looked quite shocked. And then Tommy is so annoying in the way he proposes. If he proposed at the top of his voice, I should not mind so much. That might produce some effect on the public. But he does it in a horrid confidential way. When Tommy wants to be romantic he talks to one just like a doctor. I am very fond of Tommy, but his methods of proposing are quite out of date. I wish, Gertrude, you would speak to him, and tell him that once a week is quite often enough to propose to any one, and that it should always be done in a manner that attracts some attention.

EVE'S DIARY
A monologue from the book by Mark Twain

NOTE: This monologue is reprinted from Eve's Diary. Mark Twain. New York: Harper & Brothers, 1906.

EVE: We are getting along very well now, Adam and I, and getting better and better acquainted. He does not try to avoid me any more, which is a good sign, and shows that he likes to have me with him. That pleases me, and I study to be useful to him in every way I can, so as to increase his regard. During the last day or two I have taken all the work of naming things off his hands, and this has been a great relief to him, for he has no gift in that line, and is evidently very grateful. He can't think of a rational name to save him, but I do not let him see that I am aware of his defect. Whenever a new creature comes along I name it before he has time to expose himself by an awkward silence. In this way I have saved him many embarrassments. I have no defect like this. The minute I set eyes on an animal I know what it is. I don't have to reflect a moment; the right name comes out instantly, just as if it were an inspiration, as no doubt it is, for I am sure it wasn't in me half a minute before. I seem to know just by the shape of the creature and the way it acts what animal it is. When the dodo came along he thought it was a wildcat--I saw it in his eye. But I saved him. And I was careful not to do it in a way that could hurt his pride. I just spoke up in a quite natural way of pleasing surprise, and not as if I was dreaming of conveying information, and said, "Well, I do declare, if there isn't the dodo!" I explained--without seeming to be explaining--how I know it for a dodo, and although I thought maybe he was a little piqued that I knew the creature when he didn't, it was quite evident that he admired me. That was very agreeable, and I thought of it more than once with gratification before I slept. How little a thing can make us happy when we feel that we have earned it!

ENGLISH	WRITE YOUR TRANSLATION GLOSS HERE
We are getting along very well now, Adam and I, and getting better and better acquainted. He does not try to avoid me any more, which is a good sign, and shows that he likes to have me with him. That pleases me, and I study to be useful to him in every way I can, so as to increase his regard. During the last day or two I have taken all the work of naming things off his hands, and this has been a great relief to him, for he has no gift in that line, and is evidently very grateful. He can't think of a rational name to save him, but I do not let him see that I am aware of his defect. Whenever a new creature comes along I name it before he has time to expose himself by an awkward silence. In this way I have saved him many embarrassments. I have no defect like this. The minute I set eyes on an animal I know what it is. I don't have to reflect a moment; the right name comes out instantly, just as if it were an inspiration, as no doubt it is, for I am sure it wasn't in me half a minute before. I seem to know just by the shape of the creature and the way it acts what animal it is. When the dodo came along he thought it was a wildcat--I saw it in his eye. But I saved him. And I was careful not to do it in a way that could hurt his pride. I just spoke up in a quite natural way of pleasing surprise, and not as if I was dreaming of conveying information, and said, "Well, I do declare, if there isn't the dodo!" I explained-- without seeming to be explaining--how I know it for a dodo, and although I thought maybe he	

was a little piqued that I knew the creature when he didn't, it was quite evident that he admired me. That was very agreeable, and I thought of it more than once with gratification before I slept. How little a thing can make us happy when we feel that we have earned it!	

SCUBA LESSONS
A monologue from the play by Joseph Zeccola

(Photo: Crystal Atkins, photographer: Mark Benjamin)

KELLY: Did you ever wake up and know it was gonna be your day? I did. Today. First time. I woke up five minutes before my alarm went off. The sun was shining, the birds chirping, I felt warm all over and then... ... I read my horoscope. "Today is your day!!! What you dreamed about becomes real. Romance figures prominently. Musical notes involved." Okay--I don't get the musical notes thing either--but that's not the point. The point is it said today is my day. And it has been--all day!!! I got on the scale--I was five pounds thinner, and that was after getting out of the shower. On my way out the door, my manager tells me he's going to fix the broken closet in my apartment I reported six months ago. Normally I wouldn't believe it, because I have rotten luck. But I've had this feeling all day. And that's leaving out the best part of my horoscope: "Romance figures Prominently." *[She looks around the cafe.]* He's not here yet. Martin. My date.

Crystal Adkins

Actually it's a blind date. Both Dan and I have blind dates tonight. Which would normally scare me. Which is why I told Dan to meet his date here, too. I had a friend at work set us up. Raul. He's gay. We decided to meet our dates at the same place just in case they were ugly. If I knew my day was gonna be like this, I would have told him to fend for himself. He's Italian, they like those buxom women. Or at least he does. And he thinks he speaks for every guinea on the planet. He doesn't like it when I call him a guinea. *[Short pause]* Guinea. Oh. That's Dan. He likes me. But we're not. No. I mean he's sweet. We always do stuff like this together. Well not like this. We do things. We go to the movies. We go for walks--in the park or mountains. Sometimes we even hold hands. Sometimes we come here and get coffee. Well he gets coffee. I don't like coffee. Or tea. Actually I hate tea; but, we're just friends. It's hard to explain. Dan and I ... ... we just--we wouldn't get along. We bicker constantly. Dan calls me the ex-wife he never wanted. I call him evidence to the need for artificial insemination. *[Pause.]* He's really not that bad. He's just that bad for me. Dan just needs to find a woman who isn't annoyed by him. And who isn't meeting her soulmate tonight.

Did you ever wake up and know it was gonna be your day? I did. Today. First time. I woke up five minutes before my alarm went off. The sun was shining, the birds chirping, I felt warm all over and then... ... I read my horoscope. "Today is your day!!! What you dreamed about becomes real. Romance figures prominently. Musical notes involved." Okay--I don't get the musical notes thing either--but that's not the point. The point is it said today is my day. And it has been--all day!!! I got on the scale--I was five pounds thinner, and that was after getting out of the shower. On my way out the door, my manager tells me he's going to fix the broken closet in my apartment I reported six months ago. Normally I wouldn't believe it, because I have rotten luck. But I've had this feeling all day. And that's leaving out the best part of my horoscope: "Romance figures Prominently."
[She looks around the cafe.] He's not here yet. Martin. My date. Actually it's a blind date. Both Dan and I have blind dates tonight. Which would normally scare me. Which is why I told Dan to meet his date here, too. I had a friend at work set us up. Raul. He's gay. We decided to meet our dates at the same place just in case they were ugly. If I knew my day was gonna be like this, I would have told him to fend for himself. He's Italian, they like those buxom women. Or at least he does. And he thinks he speaks for every guinea on the planet. He doesn't like it when I call him a guinea.
[Short pause] Guinea. Oh. That's Dan. He likes me. But we're not. No. I mean he's sweet. We always do stuff like this together. Well not like this. We do things. We go to the movies. We go for walks--in the park or mountains. Sometimes we even hold hands. Sometimes we come here and get coffee. Well he gets coffee. I don't like coffee. Or tea. Actually I hate tea; but, we're just friends. It's hard to explain. Dan and I ... ... we just--we wouldn't get along. We bicker constantly. Dan calls me the ex-wife he never wanted. I call him evidence to the need

| for artificial insemination. *[Pause.]* He's really not that bad. He's just that bad for me. Dan just needs to find a woman who isn't annoyed by him. And who isn't meeting her soulmate tonight. | |

MRS. CAUDLE'S UMBRELLA
A monologue by Douglas William Jerrold

NOTE: This monologue is reprinted from <u>One Hundred Choice Selections</u>. Ed. Phineas Garrett. Philadelphia: Penn Publishing Co., 1897.

MRS. CAUDLE: Bah! That's the third umbrella gone since Christmas. *What were you to do?* Why, let him go home in the rain, to be sure. I'm very certain there was nothing about him that could spoil. *Take cold?* Indeed! He doesn't look like one of the sort to take cold. Besides, he'd have better taken cold than taken our umbrella. Do you hear the rain, Mr. Caudle? I say, do you hear the rain? And, as I am alive, if it isn't Saint Swithin's day! Do you hear it against the windows? Nonsense, you don't impose upon me. You can't be asleep with such a shower as that! Do you hear it, I say? Oh, you *do* hear it? Well that's a pretty flood, I think, to last for six weeks; and no stirring all the time out of the house. Pooh! don't think me a fool, Mr. Caudle. Don't insult me. *He return the umbrella?* Anybody would think you were born yesterday. As if anybody ever did return an umbrella! There--do you hear it? Worse and worse! Cats and dogs, and for six weeks--always six weeks,--and no umbrella! When I do go out, Mr. Caudle, I choose to go as a lady. Oh! that rain--if it isn't enough to break in the windows. Ugh! I look forward with dread for tomorrow. How am I to go to mother's I'm sure I can't tell. But, if I die, I'll do it. No, sir; I won't *borrow* an umbrella. No; and you shan't *buy* one. Mr. Caudle, if you bring home another umbrella, I'll throw it into the street. Ha! it was only last week I had a new nozzle put to that umbrella. I'm sure if I'd have known as much as I do now, it might have gone without one for me. Paying for new nozzles, for other people to laugh at you. Oh, it's all very well for you, you can go to sleep! You've no thought of your poor, patient wife and your own dear children. You think of nothing but lending umbrellas. Men, indeed!--call themselves lords of creation!--pretty lords, when they can't even take care of an umbrella!

ENGLISH   WRITE YOUR TRANSLATION GLOSS HERE

Bah! That's the third umbrella gone since Christmas. *What were you to do?* Why, let him go home in the rain, to be sure. I'm very certain there was nothing about him that could spoil. *Take cold?* Indeed! He doesn't look like one of the sort to take cold.

Besides, he'd have better taken cold than taken our umbrella. Do you hear the rain, Mr. Caudle? I say, do you hear the rain? And, as I am alive, if it isn't Saint Swithin's day! Do you hear it against the windows? Nonsense, you don't impose upon me. You can't be asleep with such a shower as that! Do you hear it, I say? Oh, you *do* hear it? Well that's a pretty flood, I think, to last for six weeks; and no stirring all the time out of the house. Pooh! don't think me a fool, Mr. Caudle. Don't insult me. *He return the umbrella?* Anybody would think you were born yesterday. As if anybody ever did return an umbrella! There--do you hear it? Worse and worse! Cats and dogs, and for six weeks-- always six weeks,--and no umbrella! When I do go out, Mr. Caudle, I choose to go as a lady. Oh! that rain--if it isn't enough to break in the windows. Ugh! I look forward with dread for tomorrow. How am I to go to mother's I'm sure I can't tell. But, if I die, I'll do it. No, sir; I won't *borrow* an umbrella. No; and you shan't *buy* one. Mr. Caudle, if you bring home another umbrella, I'll throw it into the street. Ha! it was only last week I had a new nozzle put to that umbrella. I'm sure if I'd have known as much as I do now, it might have gone without one for me. Paying for new nozzles, for other people to laugh at you. Oh, it's all very well for you, you can go to sleep! You've

no thought of your poor, patient wife and your own dear children. You think of nothing but lending umbrellas. Men, indeed!--call themselves lords of creation!--pretty lords, when they can't even take care of an umbrella!	

OHIO
A monologue from the play by Nick Zagone

NOTE: This monologue is reprinted with the author's permission. All inquiries should be directed to the author at: nickzagone@sbcglobal.net

JANICE: While we have a minute I thought I'd show you some paintings. This is a three part series of oils I painted called "Aliens." Which is Alien. The movie. The movie "Alien." Well, the movies. I guess the "Alien Trilogy" might be a better term. Yes! The movies with Sigourney Weaver! You've seen them, that's good. More women should see them. All women should see the Alien Trilogy. What do some sci-fi movies have to do with women you ask? Well, these simple science fiction movies could very well be the verifiable, trustworthy reflection of the struggle of the American Woman in our society over the last thirty years! Cross my heart. Each movie not only depicts the struggles of Ripley, the heroine, against the Aliens, but of Ripley the woman against man, technology, and her role in society! Oh, I know, don't get me started! These movies are the perfect measure of how far the American woman has come, and in my paintings I have chosen to represent... this. And here they are! Since the three movies span three decades I have painted three paintings to represent the sociological and political concepts that abound... in each. In my first painting which I call Alien I, you can see the decade of the 70's fully represented. Meanwhile, the Alien... seen here dressed like Annie Hall with an Asian face and a gas can... Okay. Are you with me? In the second painting...which I call Alien II, it is now the 80's. We see the male characters who have become trapped and helpless in the grips of their own technology, employ our heroine, Ripley, to fight the Alien once again. Ripley's hair is now short. She carries a gun. She fights side-by-side with the Marines. And she still looks sexy. It looks like woman is now on the same level as man. The last painting, Alien III. It is now the 90's and hope is gone. Get it? And Ripley's hair? Is now completely gone. Shaved. She has been stripped of her most cherished female characteristic. Ripley is now a living metaphor for a woman no longer trapped by her own body. She is not a woman, nor a man, nor an Alien. She has transcended it all. She is herself. As represented by Ripley bursting from the stomach of an Alien with Bill Clinton's head. *[A beat.]* I know. They're not that good.

ENGLISH   WRITE YOUR TRANSLATION GLOSS HERE

While we have a minute I thought I'd show you some paintings. This is a three part series of oils I painted called "Aliens." Which is Alien. The movie. The movie "Alien." Well, the movies. I guess the "Alien Trilogy" might	

be a better term. Yes! The movies with
Sigourney Weaver! You've seen them, that's
good. More women should see them. All
women should see the Alien Trilogy. What do
some sci-fi movies have to do with women you
ask? Well, these simple science fiction movies
could very well be the verifiable, trustworthy
reflection of the struggle of the American
Woman in our society over the last thirty
years! Cross my heart. Each movie not only
depicts the struggles of Ripley, the heroine,
against the Aliens, but of Ripley the woman
against man, technology, and her role in
society! Oh, I know, don't get me started!
These movies are the perfect measure of how
far the American woman has come, and in my
paintings I have chosen to represent… this.
And here they are! Since the three movies span
three decades I have painted three paintings to
represent the sociological and political
concepts that abound… in each. In my first
painting which I call Alien I, you can see the
decade of the 70's fully represented.
Meanwhile, the Alien… seen here dressed like
Annie Hall with an Asian face and a gas can…
Okay. Are you with me? In the second
painting...which I call Alien II, it is now the
80's. We see the male characters who have
become trapped and helpless in the grips of
their own technology, employ our heroine,
Ripley, to fight the Alien once again. Ripley's
hair is now short. She carries a gun. She fights
side-by-side with the Marines. And she still
looks sexy. It looks like woman is now on the
same level as man. The last painting, Alien III.
It is now the 90's and hope is gone. Get it?
And Ripley's hair? Is now completely gone.
Shaved. She has been stripped of her most
cherished female characteristic. Ripley is now
a living metaphor for a woman no longer
trapped by her own body. She is not a woman,
nor a man, nor an Alien. She has transcended it
all. She is herself. As represented by Ripley
bursting from the stomach of an Alien with
Bill Clinton's head. *[A beat.]* I know. They're
not that good.

THE ROMANTIC YOUNG LADY
A monologue from the play by Gregorio Martinez Sierra
(photo: Beth Applebaum, photographer: Amanda Stuhler)

NOTE: This monologue is reprinted from The Plays of G. Martinez Sierra.
G. Martinez Sierra. New York: E.P. Dutton, 1922.

DOÑA BARBARITA: I was jealous of every woman my first husband looked in the face ... and he was a portrait painter, do you remember? My second husband suffered tortures from his own jealousy ... of your grandfather. That was premature, but prophetic, for your dear grandfather was our neighbor in those days and he used to stand and look at me from his balcony. And then he in his turn tortured himself, poor man, with jealousy of my second husband, who was dead by that time to be sure ... but that only seemed to make it worse. When I think of the times I've walked into my first husband's studio, shaking all over, to see what sort of woman he was painting this time ... and how much of her, and of the times when I'd glance up at your grandfather on his balcony and let my dear second husband imagine ... God forgive me ... that I was smiling at him; and then when your grandfather would catch me looking at my poor second husband's portrait ... my first husband had painted it while they were both alive ... and if I wanted to drive him to fury, I'd only to give one sigh. Well, now they're in Heaven all three and I'm almost sorry I worried them so. *[She kisses the three pictures.]* But never forget that I was an obedient wife, gentle and loving, an angel of the fireside, an angel in crinoline. No doubt it's far nobler to "live your own life" (isn't that what you call it?) but I fear you'll never find it so amusing.

ENGLISH

ASL GLOSS

ENGLISH	ASL GLOSS
I was jealous of every woman my first husband looked in the face ... and he was a portrait painter, do you remember? My second husband suffered tortures from his own jealousy ... of your grandfather. That was premature, but prophetic, for your dear grandfather was our neighbor in those days and he used to stand and look at me from his balcony. And then he in his turn tortured himself, poor man, with jealousy of my second husband, who was dead by that time to be sure ... but that only seemed to make it worse. When I think of the times	My first husband himself painter he looked many women, woman, woman, woman, I jealous awful! You remember?

My second husband himself jealous of your grandfather. The future see early. Why? You grandfather lived nextdoor past. He past stand on balcony look-at-me.

Grandfather upset himself jealous why? Think back me with 2nd husband – silly 2nd husband dead. But grandfather imagine and torture |

I've walked into my first husband's studio, shaking all over, to see what sort of woman he was painting this time ... and how much of her, and of the times when I'd glance up at your grandfather on his balcony and let my dear second husband imagine ... God forgive me ... that I was smiling at him; and then when your grandfather would catch me looking at my poor second husband's portrait ... my first husband had painted it while they were both alive ... and if I wanted to drive him to fury, I'd only to give one sigh. Well, now they're in Heaven all three and I'm almost sorry I worried them so. *[She kisses the three pictures.]* But never forget that I was an obedient wife, gentle and loving, an angel of the fireside, an angel in crinoline. No doubt it's far nobler to "live your own life" (isn't that what you call it?) but I fear you'll never find it so amusing.	himself. I look back remember enter 1st husband's painting room jealous, shaking worried see woman he paint now – she naked? I look back remember your grandfather look-at me stand on balcony I look up know my 2nd husband jealous – I smile let 2nd husband think I affair have. I look back remember tease Grandfather I look at 2nd husband picture let Grandfather jealous. If I want him crazy I can – do –do "sigh" Now three men all dead enter heaven I sorry I force them jealous (kiss three pictures) I good wife, obey, gentle, ILY, I idea same angle of home, angel in hoop dress. You right better to "live your own life" same you say before. But not enjoy same!

MIDSUMMER NIGHTS DREAM
Hermia Act II Scene II

   Her. [*Awaking.*] Help me, Lysander, help me! do thy best
To pluck this crawling serpent from my breast.
Ay me, for pity! what a dream was here!   *140*
Lysander, look how I do quake with fear:
Methought a serpent eat my heart away,
And you sat smiling at his cruel prey.
Lysander! what! remov'd?—Lysander! lord!   *144*
What! out of hearing? gone? no sound, no word?
Alack! where are you? speak, an if you hear;
Speak, of all loves! I swound almost with fear.
No! then I well perceive you are not nigh: *148*
Either death or you I'll find immediately. [*Exit.*

DoverCards.com

ENGLISH	ASL "Gloss"
Her. [*Awaking.*] Help me, Lysander, help me! do thy best	(Wake up slowly as if from a bad dream) Lysander "L" help! Help! Do you best
To pluck this crawling serpent from my breast.	I dream snake crawl all-over "L" catch snake pull off me!
Ay me, for pity! what a dream was here!	(waking up fully) Wow! Pity myself. Terrible dream
Lysander, look how I do quake with fear:	"L" look at me I still shake fear
Methought a serpent eat my heart away,	I dream snake eat my heart
And you sat smiling at his cruel prey.	You sat watch me smile, mean!
Lysander! what! remov'd?—Lysander! lord!	"L" where go? "L" where where
What! out of hearing? gone? no sound, no word?	Maybe he can't see me call. He leave not tell me goodbye?
Alack! where are you? speak, an if you hear;	
Speak, of all loves! I swound almost with fear.	Where where show me where you go "L"
No! then I well perceive you are not nigh:	Contact me my love. I feel dizzy, weak knees so scared
Either death or you I'll find immediately. [*Exit.*	"L" not come he not here must gone I accept I search find "L" Or my death Now!

Bell, Book and Candle

By John Van Druten

This play was the original story for what later became the television show "Bewitched" The character of Miss Holroyd is a spacey, well-meaning but basically unskilled witch and the Aunt of the main character, Gillian. She is trying to help Gillian find love but her blundering isn't helping.

Why? What have I done? I only broke into his house and played tricks on his phone because he reported me to the agents. That was just to pay him out. I know, I know when you let me move in here I promised to be careful. But what harm did I do? I didn't TAKE anything. Yes. I read his letters, but it's not as if I were going to make USE of them. Though I'm tempted to now – now that he's told on me – to you. He'd never suspect, darling. Not in a million years. No matter WHAT I did. Honestly it's amazing the way people don't. Why, they don't believe there ARE such things. I sit in the subways sometimes, or in busses, and look at the people next to me, and I think: What would you say if I told you I was a witch? And I know they'd never believe it. They just wouldn't believe it. And I giggle and giggle to myself.
I will not swear on the manual to stop practicing in the house. I know you want me to but... well, YOU practice in the house. (hurt) if you make me swear, I'll move to a hotel. I've other people I can turn to you know.

Oh PLEASE don't make me swear on the manual. I swear that I will not practice witchcraft ever in this house again. So help me Tagla, Salamandrae, Brazo and Vesturiel.

I think you are very cruel.

ENGLSIH	ASL "Gloss"
Why? What have I done? I only broke into his house and played tricks on his phone because he reported me to the agents. That was just to pay him out. I know, I know when you let me move in here I promised to be careful. But what harm did I do? I didn't TAKE anything. Yes. I read his letters, but it's not as if I were going to make USE of them. Though I'm tempted to now – now that he's told on me – to you.	Why stop? I innocent me Admit His house I magic window and climb in, but he report me. Big trouble from agents I want two-finger-zap. I know know you allow me move with you. Past I promise careful will. But I not hurt nothing. I not steal nothing. Admit his letters I read. But I not use letters for magic. Tempt now – why he tell you I bad.
He'd never suspect, darling. Not in a million years. No matter WHAT I did. Honestly it's amazing the way people don't. Why, they don't believe there ARE such things. I sit in the subways sometimes, or in busses, and look at the people next to me, and I think: What would you say if I told you I was a witch? And I know they'd never believe it. They just wouldn't believe it. And I giggle and giggle to myself.	I magic him he not suspicious no. He guess I magic never one million years he not guess. Honest people clueless, amazing! People not believe witches real. Happen I sit subway or bus. I look-around see people sit-next-to-me. I imagine I tell "I'm witch!" people believe? Never! Refuse believe. I laugh, laugh, not tell them.
I will not swear on the manual to stop practicing in the house. I know you want me to but… well, YOU practice in the house. (hurt) if you make me swear, I'll move to a hotel. I've other people I can turn to you know.	Refuse! I not swear on witch book stop magic in house. I know you want me stop. Not fair! YOU magic in house. Force me swear I leave move hotel. Other people support me will PLEASE not force me swear.
Oh PLEASE don't make me swear on the manual.	I promise I not magic in house again. I promise all boss witches, T, S, B, V. I swear.
I swear that I will not practice witchcraft ever in this house again. So help me Tagla, Salamandrae, Brazo and Vesturiel.	You very mean.
I think you are very cruel.	

RENT
Character name: MAUREEN

Last night, I had a dream
I found myself in a desert called Cyberland
It was hot
My canteen had sprung a leak and I was thirsty
Out of the obis walked a cow, Elsie
I asked if she had anything to drink she said
"I am forbidden to produce milk,
In Cyberland we only drink Diet Coke (coke...coke...coke)
She said
"Only thing to do is just over the moon"
They've closed everything real down
Like barns and troths and...
Performance Spaces
And replaced it all with lies and rules and
Virtual Life... But there is a way out
Leap of faith, leap of faith, leap of faith, leap of faith
Only thing to do is jump over the moon
I gotta get outta here
It's like i'm being tied to the hood of
a yellow rental truck being packed in with fertilizer and fuel oil pushed over a cliff by a suicidal mickey mouse
I gotta gotta gotta gotta gotta gotta gotta gotta gotta gotta gotta gotta gotta gotta gotta gotta gotta gotta find a way...
to jump over the moon

ENGLISH	ASL "Gloss"
Last night, I had a dream	Last Night dream-imagine
I found myself in a desert called Cyberland	Dry area place named what? Cyber land
It was hot	Hot!
My canteen had sprung a leak and I was thirsty	Happen water bottle leak water go down I
Out of the obis walked a cow, Elsie	thirsty me empty all around – them I see cow
I asked if she had anything to drink she said	Cow name what? Elsie
"I am forbidden to produce milk,	I ask cow I thirsty, don't mind share drink?
In Cyberland we only drink Diet Coke	Cow say illegal milk can't
(coke...coke...coke)	Happen here we drink diet coke only
She said	Coke, coke, coke
"Only thing to do is jump over the moon"	Cow say
They've closed everything real down	You do do moon jump over
Like barns and troths and...	Real life closed
Performance Spaces	No barns, no food , no theaters
And replaced it all with lies and rules and	Real life replace now have lies, rules computer
Virtual Life... But there is a way out	life

Leap of faith, leap of faith, leap of faith, leap of faith Only thing to do is jump over the moon I gotta get outta here It's like i'm being tied to the hood of a yellow rental truck being packed in with fertilizer and fuel oil pushed over a cliff by a suicidal mickey mouse I gotta gotta gotta gotta gotta gotta gotta gotta gotta gotta gotta gotta gotta gotta gotta gotta gotta gotta find a way... to jump over the moon	But I know escape how Must faith – must quote jump faith" jump faith You do do moon jump over I must out out I feel same stuck tied up on top Truck, rental truck yellow inside truck? Shit, oil Happen what? Mickey Mouse push truck cliff it fall over I must out, go escape, leave, run, pow-out-of- here Go, out , leave must I must go, go go Must figure way Moon jump over

ROMEO & JULIET

JULIET: Shall I speak ill of him that is my husband?
Ah, poor my lord, what tongue shall smooth thy name
When I, thy three-hours wife, have mangled it?
But wherefore, villain, didst thou kill my cousin?
That villain cousin would have killed my husband.
Back, foolish tears, back to your native spring!
Your tributary drops belong to woe,
Which you, mistaking, offer up to joy.
My husband lives, that Tybalt would have slain;
And Tybalt's dead, that would have slain my husband.
All this is comfort; wherefore weep I then?
Some word there was, worser than Tybalt's death,
That murd'red me. I would forget it fain;
But O, it presses to my memory
Like damnèd guilty deeds to sinners' minds!
'Tybalt is dead, and Romeo--banishèd!'
That 'banishèd,' that one word 'banishèd,'
Hath slain ten thousand Tybalts. Tybalt's death
Was woe enough, if it had ended there;
Or, if sour woe delights in fellowship
And needly will be ranked with other griefs,
Why followèd not, when she said 'Tybalt's dead,'
Thy father, or thy mother, nay, or both,
Which modern lamentation might have moved?
But with a rearward following Tybalt's death,
'Romeo is banishèd'--to speak that word
Is father, mother, Tybalt, Romeo, Juliet,
All slain, all dead. 'Romeo is banishèd'--

There is no end, no limit, measure, bound,
In that word's death; no words can that woe sound.

ENGLISH	ASL "GLOSS"
Shall I speak ill of him that is my husband?	You want me say my husband evil?
Ah, poor my lord, what tongue shall smooth thy name	No! If I talk against who support will?
When I, thy three-hours wife, have mangled it?	We married only short time 3 hours
But wherefore, villain, didst thou kill my cousin?	But he killed my cousin maybe true biz evil
That villain cousin would have killed my husband.	My cousin want murder husband
Back, foolish tears, back to your native spring!	I can't stop cry cry, wish I can pull them back
Your tributary drops belong to woe,	into eyes
Which you, mistaking, offer up to joy.	Tear drops show heart break, should show
My husband lives, that Tybalt would have slain;	thrilled
And Tybalt's dead, that would have slain my husband.	My husband lives
	Almost die fight with cousin
All this is comfort; wherefore weep I then?	Cousin dead, want kill husband
Some word there was, worser than Tybalt's death,	I should feel relieved
That murd'red me. I would forget it fain;	Why I cry why?
But O, it presses to my memory	Worse hurt my heart worse than cousin dead
Like damnèd guilty deeds to sinners' minds!	Heart break I wish forget can
'Tybalt is dead, and Romeo--banishèd!'	But no! remember one word stuck
That 'banishèd,' that one word 'banishèd,'	Idea same guilty do-do stay in mind sinner
Hath slain ten thousand Tybalts. Tybalt's death	Cousin dead, husband
Was woe enough, if it had ended there;	banished (exclude)
Or, if sour woe delights in fellowship	banished worse than 10,000 cousins dead
And needly will be ranked with other griefs,	cousin die bad enough end, finish
Why followèd not, when she said 'Tybalt's dead,'	but must build up more sad
	more heart break
Thy father, or thy mother, nay, or both,	I wish they tell me cousin dead, father dead,
Which modern lamentation might have moved?	mother dead. All dead
But with a rearward following Tybalt's death,	I would cry cry cry
'Romeo is banishèd'--to speak that word	
Is father, mother, Tybalt, Romeo, Juliet,	But tell me cousin dead
All slain, all dead. 'Romeo is banishèd'--	Husband BANISHED – that one word
There is no end, no limit, measure, bound,	Means father, mother, cousin, husband, me
In that word's death; no words can that woe sound.	All killed, all dead. Husband banished
	That one owrd equal death with no end, finish not
	That one word worse than death

Luane Davis Haggerty, Ph.D.

- Interborough Repertory Theater (IRT) Co-Founder
- Rochester Institute of Technology, National Technical Institute for the Deaf Assistant Professor of Creative and Cultural Studies
- Actor
- Director
- Writer
- Educator
- ASL Interpreter
-

Luane Davis is co-founder of the Interborough Repertory Theater (IRT), a non-profit AEA Off-Off Broadway Company dedicated to inclusion and outreach to women, the disabled and other minorities. IRT is a long term member of The Alliance of Resident Theatres in New York and has been given awards and grants for their work with children, outreach programs, showcase work and Off-Broadway productions. She has been a Public Education Specialist for New York State Department of Mental Retardation Developmental Disabilities and is now an Assistant Professor at the National Technical Institute for the Deaf (NTID) at Rochester Institute of Technology in the department of Creative and Cultural Studies.

She is also the creator of the Del-Sign acting technique and Artistic Director of the Del-Sign Project in NYC, most recently profiled in Theatre Week, Village Voice and Time Out magazines. Del-Sign combines the disciplines of American Sign Language and Delsarte mime technique, opening doors of access and breaking ground for the art of performance. She has directed several of NTID'S most popular productions in this technique garnering a feature article in the *Chronicle of Higher Education* and winning the Industry's Off Off Broadway Review Award. The Del-Sign technique is an invaluable educational tool as well and Ms. Davis has been a presenter at the Theater 2000 Convention in NYC, the International Thespian Society and the Convention for American Instructors of the Deaf.

On the other side of the footlights, she has appeared on Broadway as a featured performer at Radio City Music Hall, Symphony Space. Her Off Broadway credits include all 13 of the Gilbert and Sullivan Operettas, as well as premieres of works by Robert Patrick and Joyce Carol Oates. Her regional and stock credits range from Shakespeare to Sondheim and she's been heard in a range of commercial voice overs. She won a Conde Nast #1 rating as a headliner on the American Queen, sharing the stage with Donald O'Connor, Steve Allen, Jane Meadows and Jack Jones. Ms. Davis has appeared in Rochester in GeVa Theater and at NTID's Panara Theater in the American Deaf Playwrights Festival. She has sung and signed the National Anthem to over 5,000 people at the Chase Corporate Challenge as well as at the Deaf Olympics. She has sung Jazz in New Orleans, Memphis and New York and her recent jazz CD REFLECTIONS is available at www.cdbaby.com As a writer, she is a member of the Dramatists Guild and has had five plays produced. She was awarded the Women's Midwestern Arts Council Award for her play, WOMEN OF THE AMERICAN REVOLUTION and a Pulitzer Prize nomination for WINDOWS OF THE SOUL. Her self-help book TAKING STAGE is used as an Arts Management text book and her novel the FRED-OIRSare available through www.lulu.com . She has been honored with several notable awards, among them are: Outstanding Young American , inclusion in WHO'S WHO in Theater and Governor Pataki's award for WOMEN OF ACHIEVEMENT.